Alfred Thomas Tucker Wise

Alpine Winter in its Medical Aspects

Second Edition

Alfred Thomas Tucker Wise

Alpine Winter in its Medical Aspects
Second Edition

ISBN/EAN: 9783337258429

Printed in Europe, USA, Canada, Australia, Japan

Cover: Foto ©Andreas Hilbeck / pixelio.de

More available books at **www.hansebooks.com**

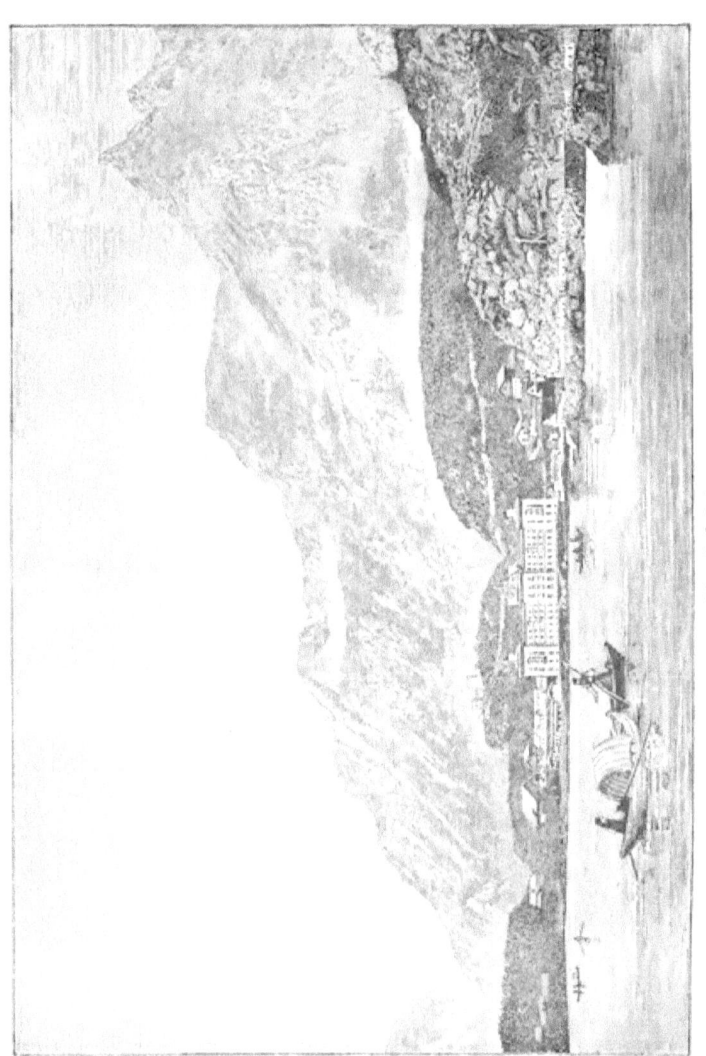

MALOJA.

ALPINE WINTER

IN ITS MEDICAL ASPECTS:

WITH NOTES ON

DAVOS PLATZ, WIESEN, ST. MORITZ,

AND

THE MALOJA.

BY

A. TUCKER WISE, M.D., L.R.C.P., M.R.C.S.,

Formerly Visiting Physician to the Infirmary for Consumption, Margaret St., Cavendish Sq.;
Physician to the Western General Dispensary; Honorary Medical Officer to the
Kilburn and Maida Vale Dispensary;
House Physician, House Surgeon, and Resident Obstetric Officer, St. Mary's Hospital, London;
Member of the Harveian Society; Fellow of the Royal Meteorological Society, &c.;
Author of "Davos Platz, and the Effects of High Altitude on Phthisis," "Wiesen as a Health
Resort in Early Phthisis," &c., &c.

SECOND EDITION.

LONDON:
J. & A. CHURCHILL, NEW BURLINGTON STREET, W.

1885.

LONDON :
T. BANKS, STEAM PRINTER, GREAT WINDMILL STREET, W.

PREFACE TO THE SECOND EDITION.

The First Edition of this book appeared under the title "Alpine Winter Cure," this has now been changed to "Alpine Winter in its Medical Aspects."

The progress which has been made in the study of micro-organisms, draws attention to the immense importance of the quality of air breathed within doors at all stations frequented by persons in search of health. This is of great moment in the Alpine winter stations, where so many hours out of the twenty-four have to be spent in the house. The climate does not admit of free ventilation by open windows, and consequently, in spite of the general examples of remarkable cures, many of the advantages of breathing mountain air are curtailed unless efficient means are adopted to effect constant changes of air indoors.

As the Belgian enterprise of building the Maloja Kursaal is the first true attempt to construct a residence in these cold climates, with an efficient and costly system of ventilation and warming, *without the aid of stoves*, a special portion of the book has been devoted to its description. It is to be hoped that the example set in sanitary matters, in this undertaking, may be imitated by other hotel-companies and proprietors, so that the ventilation and drainage of dwellings may meet with the scrutiny which such important points demand.

In addition to the steps taken for renewing the air in this new establishment by artificial means, a plan has been adopted, at my suggestion, of introducing ozone into the building. This is effected by electricity in connection with the electric lighting of the Kursaal, the fall of the river Inn being the motor-force employed for the purpose. It is also possible, by a simple contrivance, to volatilise remedial agents in the hot air of the ventilation tubes, and distribute the drug in any single chamber without infecting other rooms by its odour. The extreme cleanness of the internal atmosphere, however, renders such a proceeding quite superfluous, as the frequent changes in the whole building, produce with the ozonised currents, a state of purity perhaps never before attained in any large habitation. Coupled with the large quantities of solar light received by the Maloja the results on the quality of the blood (especially in anæmic persons dwelling at these altitudes) can only be highly beneficial.

The sudden change which the air, sunlight, and scenery of the mountains give to physical and mental depression is little short of marvellous; marked improvement usually setting in after a short stay: unlike the results of a sojourn in the South, where not unfrequently the full force of "change" is unperceived until a return is made to the cooler climate at home.

The intention in the present volume is to exhibit the remarkable curative and health-giving properties of Alpine climate in their true light, avoiding exaggeration or an omission of those minor details termed "drawbacks," so necessary to be pourtrayed in the consideration of any foreign or home health-resort.

The omission of the analysis of a mineral water, in the present edition, is by reason of the subject being in abeyance. Mr. Hainean, who professes to be an expert as regards discovering the situation of mineral springs, declares that a chalybeate water exists on the property of the Maloja. During his visit in the year 1883, water collected by him and purporting to be derived from the Maloja, was analysed by Professor Reichhardt, of Jena University; on the strength of these assurances, coupled with the arrangements for constructing an *établissement de bains*, I gave in my last edition the analysis of the water. Owing to the sum demanded by Mr. Hainean, for disclosing the locality of the water, not meeting with the approval of the Company no steps were taken to captivate the spring, and other matters of importance replaced the further consideration of the subject.

Some suggestions having been made that a short description of the excursions in the vicinity of the Maloja would be welcomed by many visitors to the Kursaal, I have subjoined a brief sketch of the various walks and drives. Although this is a departure from the main theme of the book, it is added for the purpose of affording information to those who desire to make use of it. Further acquaintance with outlying districts can be gleaned from the J.E.M. Guide to Switzerland, which is a serviceable and easily understood handbook.

A. T. W.

Haute Engadine,
July, 1885.

CONTENTS.

	PAGE
INTRODUCTION ...	9

CHAPTER I.

The Health Resorts — Davos Platz and Dörfli, Wiesen, St. Moritz, Pontresina, Samaden, Silvaplana, Andermatt, Arosa ... 13

CHAPTER II.

Water and Soil — Atmosphere in the High Alps — Ventilation of the Hotels — Dust — Therapeutic Effects of "Cold" — Sunlight — Barometric Pressure — Increased Combustion — Ozone — Oxygen 23

CHAPTER III.

"Cold" as a Sensation and as Temperature — Characteristics of Alpine Climate and its Effects on the Vascularity of the Lungs and on Nutrition ... 41

CHAPTER IV.

The "Drawbacks" of Alpine Winter Stations — Coire as an Intermediate Resting-place 49

CHAPTER V.

Winter Clothing — Diet in the Swiss Alps — Exercise, Meals, Sleep, &c. 59

CHAPTER VI.

The Maloja — Necessity for Sanitary Precautions in the High Valleys of Switzerland — The Hôtel-Kursaal de la Maloja — Drainage — The Plateau: its Mountain-Screen — Rarity of the Föhn Wind — Duration of Sunlight, and Advantages of Solar Rays in Anæmia

—Level Promenades and Healthy Amusements—Facility in Reaching Lower Levels from the Maloja—A Description of the Heating and Ventilating Arrangements used in the Hôtel-Kursaal—Summer Alpine Climate for Early Phthisis—Duration of the "Summer Season," and Length of Time Necessary for Renovation of Lost Health—Contra-Indications of High Elevations—Healthy Indoor Amusements possible in the Maloja Hotel 72

Tabular Comparison of the Health Resorts in Grisons—Comparison in Sunshine of the Maloja with other Stations, and Mean Temperature 88

The Journey from England 91

The Meteorology of the Maloja—Drying Power of the Air ... 94

Meteorological Observations taken in the Maloja during Winter 100

Hygrometric Comparison of the Maloja with Egypt ... 110

Summary of Meteorological Observations taken at Maloja during Winter ... ... , ... 111

Attractions in the Neighbourhood of the Maloja ... 113

INTRODUCTION.

The first impression on beholding a snow-clad landscape in a cold climate during fine weather is one of surprise and admiration. Conscious of excessive cold by external appearances rather than by disagreeable sensations of chilliness, one almost doubts the reality of the low temperature. A bright sun and blue sky overhead, a clear and quiet atmosphere, distant sounds transmitted to the ear through the still air, combine with the charms of the scenery to produce such buoyancy of spirits that a man is braced and invigorated for almost any exertion.

An Englishman inured to a damp and windy climate, and with an inherent love for outdoor sports and exercises, feels new life and energy as he views the glassy expanse of a frozen Canadian lake surrounded by dense forest, or makes his way through the rugged boulders and pines of Nova Scotia. A blazing sun above would almost persuade him it was summer, whilst he recognises the sing-song of the sleigh-bells in the distance, miles away it may be, and tastes the keen atmosphere of a bright winter's day.

There may be several degrees of frost, but there is seldom that piercing raw cold experienced in England, which depends mainly on the quantity of moisture in the air and the force of the wind rather than on the pitch of the thermometer.

The effects on the Anglo-Saxon race of living in a cold climate may be seen in Canada and some of the Northern States of America, where the race is physically superior and more vigorous than that of the parent stock. This, no doubt, depends to a large extent on the mode of life, quality of food, and outdoor exercise taken, in addition to an artificial selection of species in emigration. Nevertheless, such is the fact that these cold climates, with wide ranges of temperature, harden the European constitution by invigorating the whole frame, and rendering the body less susceptible to changes in temperature, privation, or disease.

What the eventual results will be on the English race by the growth of population and consequent increase of indoor employment, it is difficult to foretell. Certain it is that dwellers in large towns, *employées* in factories, workshops, warehouses, offices, &c., are not exposed to the most favourable conditions of life in regard to health and robust development; and although the "survival of the fittest" will select the strongest and most suitable being to withstand what may almost be termed the ravages of civilisation, even the selected one will scarcely be improved by the deteriorating effects of over-crowding, impure air, improper food, want of sunlight and equable exercise of all the organs of the body.

With examples before us of the health-giving properties of cold regions, it may seem an oversight that cold climates as "change" never received the attention they merited until within recent years.

One of the first to foreshadow the track which is now being pursued by many of the leaders of medicine in England, France, and Germany, was Dr. Bodington, a practitioner in Warwickshire, who recommended "dry, frosty air" in the treatment of pulmonary consumption. In a small *brochure*, published by him forty-five years ago on this subject, he said: "To live in and breathe freely the open air, without being deterred by the wind or weather, is one important and essential remedy in arresting its progress—one about which there appears to have generally prevailed a groundless alarm less the consumptive patient should take cold . . . The abode of the patient should be in an airy house in the country—if on an eminence, the better. The neighbourhood chosen should be dry and high; the soil generally of a light loam, a sandy, or gravelly bottom. The atmosphere is in such situations comparatively free from fogs and dampness. The patient ought never to be deterred by the state of the weather from exercise in the open air; if wet and rainy, a covered vehicle should be employed, with open windows. The cold is never too severe for the consumptive patient in this climate. The cooler the air which passes into the lungs the greater will be the benefit the patient will derive. *Sharp, frosty days in the winter season* are most favourable. The application of cold, pure air to the interior surface of the lungs is the most powerful sedative that can be applied, and does more to promote the healing and closing of cavities and ulcers of the lungs than any other means that can be employed . . . Many persons are alarmed and deterred from taking much exercise in the open air from the circumstance of their coughing much on their first emerging from the warm room of a house, but this shows that the air of the room was too warm, not that the common atmosphere was too cold." As adjuncts, he advocated the use of milk, wine, and generous diet. (a) In these remarkable sentences are clearly signalised the indications for residence at such health resorts as the high Swiss Valleys, and they anticipate in an unmistakable manner the treatment of pulmonary disease or weakness, by what is now termed somewhat euphoniously, " the high altitude cure."

This English practitioner appears to have been the first, or among the first, to introduce to notice as a therapeutic agent " dry, frosty air," which has proved itself to be a remedy of practical value and application in the treatment of disease.

(a) " Essay on the Treatment and Cure of Pulmonary Consumption." By George Bodington. 1840.

In more recent years Dr. Hermann Weber, with eventual success, drew attention to high, cold altitudes as presenting favourable conditions during winter months for the arrest or amelioration of phthisis. To him undoubtedly belongs the credit of having brought the subject prominently before the profession in a clear and intelligible manner, with results on patients who had wintered in the mountains. In 1864 Dr. Hermann Weber wrote: "The question of the influence of Alpine Climate—*i.e.*, localities in Switzerland elevated beyond 5,000 feet above the level of the sea—on the tendency to consumption, and on the very first stage of this disease, is one of such vast importance that I cannot help asking for the co-operation of the whole medical profession in its further examination and decision." It may appear surprising that so many years elapsed before the medical profession began to take notice of climates with low temperature. In England this can be readily accounted for, as probably the majority of persons would judge a low temperature from their own experience of cold in the mother country. For about seven or eight years Davos Platz has attracted large numbers of *poitrinaires*, and from reports published by English physicians at home the efficacy of mountain air in some cases of phthisis is now undeniable. (*a*)

As may be expected, there are numerous sheltered spots in Switzerland where health may be sought with advantage, and where the benefits of living amongst a scanty population at a high altitude are associated with clean air and sunlight.

(*a*) Dr. Clifford Allbutt, *Lancet*, 1879; Dr. C. Theodore Williams, International Medical Congress Transactions, 1881; Dr. Burney Yeo, "Health Resorts and their Uses;" Dr. Drysdale, *British Medical Journal*, 1882; Dr. Marcet, Symes Thompson, Professor Jaccoud of Paris, and others.

ALPINE WINTER STATIONS.

CHAPTER I.

Davos Platz, Wiesen, and St. Moritz, Pontresina, Samaden and Silvaplana.

The district of Davos (an elevated valley of the Canton des Grisons, in Switzerland) extends to about fourteen miles in length, and contains between 3,000 and 4,000 inhabitants. The three miles of valley, with the health-resorts Davos Platz and Dörfli, has an altitude of 5,100 feet, and is surrounded by Alps ranging to 9,000 and 10,000 feet above sea-level. This portion of the valley is effectually sheltered from the north and west winds; rather less so from the south and east. The larger village, Platz, is situated on the north-western side of the valley, and consists of hotels, "pensions," and shops. Of these there are four or five large hotels, seven or eight smaller ones, and several houses affording fair accommodation.

Some years ago the place was frequented principally by Germans and Swiss, but in recent times many English and French have wintered there, also Belgians, Russians, Spaniards, Dutch, and even Americans.

The scenery is picturesque and grand to a stranger in Switzerland, although somewhat limited in extent, the breadth of the valley being from 500 to 1,000 yards across. Numerous pine trees cover the steep slopes, and a winding stream, the "Landwasser," which is now undergoing canalisation, receives the overflow from a lake situated to to the N.E. of Davos Dörfli, is fed by numerous mountain rivulets, and acts as the main recipient for the drainage of Davos Platz.

The soil is dry and thin, excepting the central portion or bed of the valley, where it is of a peaty character Nearly the whole extent of land is used for cattle-grazing and hay, and the sides of the valley are quite free from surface moisture.

Lateral dales—Fluela, Dischma and Sertig—lead into the main floor of the Davos Valley and, afford pleasant walks and excursions when the snow is not too deep. Skating and "coasting" are the prime amusements as with all the other Alpine winter resorts. Those who are not strong enough for these exertions, take walks, sit in the sun on balconies, and amuse themselves on their own resources. Crowded rooms with a smoky or stale atmosphere must of necessity be shunned if the winter visitor be in quest of health.

The present system of drainage has undergone alteration, none too soon, as within the last two or three years the increase in the winter population of Davos has been so large that this subject has forced itself on the notice of those most interested in attracting visitors to the place. It is a duty a successful health-resort owes to its *clientèle* to be liberal in any outlay relating to sanitation, the disregard of which will inevitably be a false economy in the end. A costly effort has been made in the present instance, that adds greatly to the attractiveness of Davos as a sanatorium and reflects great credit on those who originated the scheme. As far as external drainage is concerned it cannot be denied that the town now stands amongst the first rank of health-resorts, and in appearance presents a cleanly and favourable contrast to what it did formerly. The roads in summer and winter are well swept, many paths are available for short or long walks, and what may be styled the metropolis of Alpine stations now assumes an aspect of surprising neatness combined with not unmerited pretensions to some beauty. It is impossible for one who has known the locality for even a few years, not to be struck with the many vast improvements the place has undergone. Hotels have been enlarged and added to; new ones built, and handsome villas erected. The Kurhaus of Mr. Holsboer which nearly every year shows some important supplement to the main building, is now with its theatre-salon, large café, handsome recreation rooms, and the construction of a winter-garden, one of the finest hôtels in Switzerland.

The spacious billiard and smoking rooms of the Belvedere, also deserve notice, as they will undoubtedly conduce to the health and comfort of the smoking portion of society. A new and plentiful water supply has also been brought into the town from the Fleula Valley.

Davos, however, like all the winter stations with the exception of Maloja, is not conspicuous in being provided with efficient house ventilation. It is true that the Kurhaus possesses a calorifère which ventilates the café, theatre-salon, &c., with fresh warm air, and that another hotel is fitted with Tobin's tubes in the salons; but the latter system is scarcely suited to Alpine winter climate, and the former is only applied to a limited part of the house in which it is placed.

No one has at any time seriously made the attempt to uphold Davos as faultless; nevertheless, in the present instance, it will serve a very convenient purpose to recognise, in the well-known Alpine station a suitable standard for comparison. A great deal has been said for and against the place, both by those who understood something of the climate, and by others who based their observations on short visits, or on accounts gleaned second-hand. In this way although some error has crept in, much truth and information has been elicited, greatly to the benefit of those who had never seen the place, and who have eventually experienced the curative properties of its climate.

The reputation of the little Alpine town although of many years standing, did not begin to grow with any very great rapidity until a well-known Englishman, now for some years a resident in Davos, visited the place for his own health; his experiences and friendship towards the valley have probably done more for its true appreciation by the English public, than the efforts of any other person who has interested himself on mountain health resorts.

Some misunderstanding still prevails on the problem of "cold" as a sensation, many believing that the low temperature must necessarily be unbearable, and the thought of being surrounded with snow for the whole winter awakens visions of peril to invalids. The results which have been obtained at Davos on patients with pulmonary complaints have been highly satisfactory, and even remarkable. Dr. C. Theodore Williams, who has published the details of many cases, has shown that the principal features noticed in persons who have undergone the Alpine cure, are unusual expansion of the chest, gain in flesh, and improvement in sanguification.

DAVOS DÖRFLI lies at the entrance to the Fluela Pass, about one mile from Platz in the direction of the Davoser See, is a few feet higher, and being situated opposite the Fluela Valley, receives the morning sun earlier than Davos Platz, but at the same time loses it sooner during the afternoon. In other respects no great differences exist as to climate.

Davos, like all the other mountain resorts in the Grisons can be reached by diligence from Coire, at which place a few days may be spent *en route* with benefit. Landquart, the railway station in advance of Coire, is nearer Davos, but the

VIEW OF WIESEN.

hotel accommodation is not very good, and a stay there could scarcely be made with any comfort. In winter the post leaves Coire at 7 a.m., passes Lenz at noon, where a rest is made for dinner; at 1 p.m. arrives at Wiesen, and 4 p.m. Davos Platz. From Landquart the diligence leaves at 1.10 p.m., and, traversing the Prättigau Valley, gets into Davos at 8 o'clock, the distance being twenty-nine miles instead of thirty-four miles from Coire; but the Landwasser route from the latter place is well worth seeing, and the opportunity should not be missed of travelling over an interesting and wonderful road.

WIESEN (4,771 ft. above sea-level from Dufour's trigonometrical measurements).

This small village stands about twenty-four miles from Chûr (Coire), on the picturesque Landwasser route. About 11 miles further on, after presenting several structural difficulties and passing through the Zuge gorge, the road winds into Davos.

The position of Wiesen exhibits many peculiarities and advantages as an Alpine health resort in winter. Situated on the slope of the Wiesener Alp, facing south and protected on the N. and E. by mountain ranges of 8,000 ft. and 10,000 ft. (Sandhubel, Foppa, Alteingrat, Leidbachhorn), it is effectually screened from the cold winds of winter. Sheltered equally on the southern and western aspect by the Buhlenhorn and huge Stulsergrat (8,390 ft.), the Tinzenhorn (10,278 ft.), and Piz St. Michel (10,374 ft.), and continuing the circle by the Motta Palusa, Piz Toisa and Piz Curvèr (9,760 ft.), a land-locked region is formed, radiant in winter with dazzling sunbeams. A thousand feet below is the Landwasser chafing through a narrow course to join the Albula, a mile or so beyond.

Covering the slopes are innumerable pine trees. The

odour from these is frequently perceived by new comers, and the antiseptic vapours exhaled presumably contribute to cure. The most noteworthy feature of the vicinity is an extensive plateau partially filling up the N.W. side of the basin, and jutting out towards the centre, forming an excellent and picturesque promenade. The view from the border of this plateau is seldom excelled on a small scale. Far down at one's feet is seen the floor of the gorge, with the rushing of the Landwasser audible. A peep at the Albula Valley is gained, and beyond rises the Curvér. On the left lies the little village of Jenisberg, the Stulsergrat towering above. Behind to the east is the Alteingrat, Leidbachhorn, &c., and on the right the two hotels separated from the plateau by a small vale down which the road descends to the Züge, passing the Känzeli waterfall.

Distant 11 miles from Davos, 334 ft. lower in altitude, and with a different contour of land, slight modifications in the meteorological details may be anticipated; whilst the general character of a cold, bracing, and stimulating climate is maintained. The chief points of variation from Davos are—its position on the side of a hill, sparser population, slightly higher and more equable temperature, with perhaps a little less wind. Wiesen may be considered to be about 2 or 3 degrees warmer than Davos, and, although an increase of mean temperature might lead to the belief that dangers would arise from thaws recurring, the periods of liability to actual snow-melting seldom take place with more frequency than in the latter valley. The intense heat of the sun sometimes renders parts of the main road damp under-foot when the snow is discoloured, but this could be greatly remedied by removing or covering all dirty patches as soon as formed. The plan of cleaning the roads in this manner is adopted at Davos, and would no doubt, be undertaken at Wiesen if the visitors demanded it.

With a higher mean temperature, of course the winter is

shorter compared with Davos:—this might be two or three weeks at the commencement of cold weather, and about the same at the termination of the winter. During the worst time of snow-melting in Davos (which happens either in March or April, according to the mildness or severity of the season), Wiesen clears of snow rapidly; and there being no marshy valley below, like at Davos when the snow melts, injurious consequences, if any, proceeding from evaporation are avoided. The hard frosts at night during this period depend much on terrestrial radiation and gravitation of cold air; the larger sky expanse presented to the Davos Valley favours the former, whilst the situation of the village is low. The bad part of the winter season is then prolonged, as the warmth of mid-day and afternoon causes a thaw: the evening and night change the wet snow into ice, and so delay its speedy disappearance. An early clearance of snow makes Wiesen a desirable locality for a change from Davos towards the end of the season. Or, by judiciously-timed transits from one place to the other, much of the bad weather can be escaped at either station in the months of October and March. The journey can be made within two hours, and if a tolerably fine day be selected, little risk is incurred, even in an open sleigh. Covered sleighs may be chosen; but with plenty of wraps, in bright weather an open vehicle is much to be preferred. Neither would it be at all a perilous test if the experiment were made of sending cases here when Davos was found to be unsuitable for them. If satisfactory progress were not induced, the patient would be spared the long drive to Chûr or Landquart. On the other hand, the advisability of making a rapid descent from a high altitude to the low lands, even for convalescents is questionable. Many patients, when leaving Davos for the plains, lose much of the ground they have gained, in consequence, it may be, of the fatigues of travelling, exposure to windy or damp weather, neglect of ordinary precautions or care in personal management.

ST. MORITZ.—Leaving the Davos Valley with its three stations—Davos Dörfli, Davos Platz, and Wiesen—three passes are available for a journey to the Engadine,—viz., the Fluela (7,890 feet), Albula (7,582 feet), and the Julier (7,504 feet). Strange as it may seem to those ignorant of the winter climate of these regions, a passage fraught with but little risk can be undertaken in the depth of winter, and the journey to St. Moritz or the Maloja made in one day, even by persons who are not in robust health. It is advisable however to break the journey either at Zernetz or Zuz. Many change their *locale* in this way, and when tired of one place seek the novelty and freshness of new quarters. There seems to be no objection to the practice, always provided the wanderer is in a fit state of health for the trip. St. Moritz lies in the Upper Engadine, over 6,000 feet above the level of the sea, is surrounded by lofty mountains, and fairly well sheltered from wind; it possesses the climatic characteristics of an Alpine health resort; the air is similar in quality and effects to that of other Alpine stations. Situated nearly 1,000 feet higher than Davos Platz, the barometric pressure is lessened to about 3 lbs. on the square inch, instead of about 2¼ lbs. at at the latter place. The winter season is longer, and a larger quantity of snow generally falls. Dr. Burney Yeo represented the advantages of this cold and dry climate in 1866, but at that period the high lands in Switzerland were not appreciated as they are now, and the experiment of sending patients there failed through a misunderstanding of the requirements of such cases.

Since then Dr. Symes Thompson has written an interesting brochure on winter residence at St. Moritz, embodying his experiences of the place and of the progression of several pulmonary cases, which he had sent there with marked benefit.

Two hotels are open to receive those who winter at St. Moritz, two ice rinks are in constant use, and several tracks are kept in good order for coasting and tobogganing.

PONTRESINA.—(5,915 feet), about three miles east of St. Moritz, at the foot of the Bernina pass, has a few visitors during winter-time, but it is mostly in the summer months that this attractive spot is frequented. The chief features of Pontresina is its sunlight. The village being placed on the slope, and having a magnificent mountainous but comparatively open view to the east and south, receives the first rays of the sun at 8.10 a.m., and 8.30 a.m., during December and January; whilst the sunset varies in these months from 3.5 p.m., to 3.30 p.m. The air is bracing and dry; the day-temperature is said to be about the same as Davos.

SAMADEN (5,600 feet).—The principal village in the Upper Engadine containing over 300 inhabitants and several shops, has been patronised by a few visitors in winter, mostly as a change from other resorts. Skating rinks are kept in good order and level walks are available. This spot may be said to have entered a claim to be considered an Alpine winter station as well as Silvaplana (5,958 feet), situated below the Julier Pass, and fronting the meadows which divide the lakes of Camfer and Silvaplana. The splendid mountainous views of the valley of the Inn surround both these villages, and their climate varies but little from other parts of the Upper Engadine.

Another place which has been set forth as a winter health resort is Andermatt (4,738 feet), situated in the Urseren Valley. From the unusual facilities offered by the St. Gothard line, this spot deserves to be noticed, being only 29 hours from London, with a drive of less than an hour for mounting from Göschenen. The position of this locality is excellent for convenience in travelling either to England or to the Riviera, if the mountain air is found to be unsuitable, but no personal experiences can be given here extending over sufficient time to warrant an opinion on its meteorology, or of its fitness for a winter station.

One of the most picturesque little spots in the Grisons—
"that mysteriously hidden wrinkle in the stern grey hills,
with its fairy lakes, solemn pine-forests, and emerald
meadows"—Arosa; must not be omitted from notice.
Although no strangers are known to have wintered there,
reliable accounts seem to point to its being the perfection
of winter climate. In summer the few inns are filled with
Swiss fugitives from the heat of the plains near Coire, who
preserve the secret of the unassuming beauty and charming
climate of the concealed nook. Arosa is reached by a
bridle path from Langwies, 2½ hours on foot. The construction of a road from Langwies or from Coire would soon
develop Arosa into a well-patronised abode. One portion of
the valley stands at an altitude of 6,207 feet above the sea-level, the whole area appears well-protected from all winds,
but as regards sunlight in the depth of winter, no observations
have been noted.

CHAPTER II.

Water and Soil—Atmosphere in the High Alps.—Ventilation of the Hotels.—Dust.—Therapeutic Effects of Cold, Sunlight, and Barometric Pressure.—Oxygen.—Ozone.

Water and Soil.—The water supply of the dwellings at all the high level stations is upland surface water, and appears to be of wholesome and excellent quality. It falls on the extensive summits and slopes of lofty mountains, mostly as snow, and undergoes filtration in its descent to the valleys, where it makes its appearance in small streams and springs. The rivulets selected to supply the houses are protected from cattle, &c., and the water conveyed in pine-tree tubes and iron pipes to the hotels. In winter it is constantly running to prevent the pipes freezing. The likelihood of contamination is then at a minimum, as no storage takes place in the houses, nor are there any habitations above the level or in the vicinity of the mountain streams. The water itself is without odour or flavour, and has a bright sparkling appearance from the carbonic acid taken up in the interstices of the rocky soil, through which the springs percolate. Although deprived of its oxygen in winter, by freezing, when falling as snow, it becomes sufficiently aërated in its course to the lower elevations. At Wiesen the water is drawn from sandstone, which makes it considerably softer than if obtained from the Dolomite limestone, as is generally the case at these levels. An analysis has been made of the water at Davos Platz, by Charles P. Holland, F.C.S., of Manchester, who found a somewhat considerable proportion of magnesium carbonate (4·506 gr. to the gallon), but considered the water to be exceptionally pure.

The condition and nature of the soil in the Swiss mountains, and its bearings to health, present an interesting subject of study, but one which it is impossible to deal with, at any length, in the limits of the present work. One or two of the salient features connected with the temperature, and quality of the land must not, however, be passed over.

The soil of these mountain pastures is thin, of a rich, fertile character, and absorbs roughly 1·4 (a) times its weight of water, underneath is the solid rock, mostly Dolomite limestone, except in the centre and at the edges of the valleys or ravines, where lie the moraines of ancient glaciers composed of rubbish or deep earth, intermixed with smooth blocks of rock and pebbles.

From the steep declivities on which moisture falls no injurious collection of water can take place. The drainage both of the surface and subsoil is rapid and effective. Being also of shallow depth, the danger arising from a heavy rainfall pressing up effluvia from the deeper strata is obviated; and having also no stagnant underground sheet of water, the evolution of organic emanations, forwarded by constant moisture, is not aided; or if these decompositions do occur, it is probable that absorption of their deleterious properties, is mainly affected by contact with comparatively dry earth. Vegetation also, as short thick grass covering the slopes, speedily absorbs the products of decomposition. But the condition of the land with which we are principally concerned during the winter season, takes on altogether a changed aspect, and one which until recently has attracted little attention. Uninterruptedly covered with snow for about four months during the year, the ground itself assumes the nature

(·) 2,500 grms. of soil taken from a garden at Wiesen and dried, weighed 1,850 grms. On being wetted again and allowed to drain, weighed 2,600 grms.

of "sub-soil," whilst the layer of thick snow above the actual service, modifies in a marked degree the effects of telluric influence.

Atmosphere.—As the purity, freshness, and stimulating properties of the air are important points for consideration, attention must be directed to its particular characters of humidity, temperature, barometric pressure, sunlight, wind, &c., &c.

The quantity of moisture in the atmosphere affecting the rate of evaporation from the lungs and skin is a point which requires much consideration; but at present observations have been so limited that we have not much data to go upon. Certainly, warm moist air, is sometimes very grateful to cases of congestion and irritability of the bronchial tubes; but a more permanent condition of moisture, of which our English winter affords an example, undoubtedly has an injurious influence on the majority of lung diseases; the watery vapour abstracting an undue amount of heat from the respiratory tract, and giving rise to catarrhs, coughs, or perhaps inflammations. It is a generally accepted fact that dampness of soil, apart from hereditary tendency, favours the development of phthisis. This dampness supplying the atmosphere with large quantities of moisture, shows what an important observation in climatic influences "humidity" becomes, in its results on the mitigation or development of many diseases. Now, it may be expected that in places where the surface formation is favourable for the rapid escape of surface water, where dry snow covers the ground, and the rainfall is slight, the reverse of this condition may be expected. Such is the case in the high altitudes of Switzerland; although an occasional thaw or fall of snow may saturate the air with moisture, the actual quantity of watery vapour held in suspension during winter time is extremely small, from the fact that air, at a low temperature can contain but little.

C

What the precise pathological effects are, of the habitual breathing of moist air is not yet quite clear; but Miquel has clearly affirmed that microbes are not found to be so numerous in moist weather at the Montsouris Observatory, Paris, as during dry weather; nor are they present at any time in the actual vapour of water.

As regards phthisis, however, Haviland's map shows plainly that the distribution of that malady is in favour of damp places. (a) Excessive cooling of a part of the respiratory tract from moisture, on account of the conduction of heat being more free (b) in a damp atmosphere, is frequently experienced breathing a cold London fog, the sensation of cold being then felt some times as far down the trachea as the notch of the sternum, and even lower. The result on the skin is to abstract an undue amount of heat, and retard the normal evaporation of waste products, thereby throwing more work on the lungs and kidneys. Although there is a diminished death-rate from phthisis in some parts of Scotland and Ireland, where excessive moisture prevails, the people there are mostly employed in out-door pursuits, which makes up for a great deal in the matter of health; but if a phthisical patient courted extreme ventilation in a damp climate the result would not be so satisfactory as exposure to drier sur-

---

(a) During the progress of cutting the St. Gothard Tunnel the workmen employed were exposed to a *high* temperature (80° to 90° F.) and an excessively damp atmosphere. Their health in consequence, suffered severely, one of the principal complaints being accompanied by an intestinal parasite. Catarrhs with unusual dyspnœa were constant, and the colour and appearance of the men indicated imperfect aëration of the blood, and consequent anæmia. Their strength and appetite failed them, and the body temperature was raised. There was great mortality also amongst the horses used within the tunnel.

(b) It takes a great deal more heat to raise the temperature of watery vapour than that of dry air, the apparent specific heat of which is, according to Regnault, ·2379 with pressure constant. Specific heat of vapour of water ·4750. Water 1·000, all at 32 deg. Fah.

roundings. Perhaps it is hardly necessary to mention that air containing less than 35 per cent. of moisture, with a temperature of 60° Fahr. is too dry for health, and might give rise to irritation of the air passages.

The freedom, or otherwise, from micro-organisms, mechanical irritants, noxious gases, or animal exhalations, necessitates but little discussion, as it is well know that the presence of these contaminations renders the air impure in proportion to their quantity.

The localities under consideration are shut in by high mountains, glaciers, and snow-fields; and however laden with organisms currents of air may be, it is not impossible that distant winds may be partially or wholly sterilised by becoming attenuated and cooled to a low temperature in their passage towards these valleys.

Ventilation.—Intimately connected with the subject of pure air is that of ventilation. Receiving, as it does, some scientific attention, many persons would be led to expect that a perfect system existed in any place laying claim to the appellation of "health resort." This is by no means the case generally in Switzerland. Like elsewhere, much depends on the individual as to the amount of air which he considers advantageous. In his private rooms he may exercise discretion at will; but in corridors, dining and sitting-rooms, and especially in smoking-rooms, a difficulty always presents itself. Deserving as the subject is of the greatest consideration in the Alps, it is to be regretted that so little real attention is paid to it. The purity of air in the interior of dwellings, both in health and disease, and especially in the treatment of chest affections, demands every scrutiny when we take into account the number of hours spent indoors. On the shortest day of mid-winter the sun remains but five or six hours in the valleys, therefore delicate persons must be content to pass

19 or 20 hours in the house. (a) It is obvious that some of the benefit derived from open air exposure will then be neutralised unless constant currents of fresh air are supplied for respiration.

Dust.—The great depth of snow buries all impurities, the noxious emanations of which are destroyed or lie dormant until the spring thaw. Frequent falls of snow during the winter keep any surface refuse, as it were, below ground, and assist to free the atmosphere also, from aërial germs and mechanical irritants, fixing them in a freezing medium; the former being destroyed or absorbed by the soil and vegetation, at the time of thaw; the latter being washed into, and mixed with the earth. Under these circumstances it is apparent that the air above is as pure as Nature can possibly produce it—clean, dry, calm, and laden with balsamic vapours from the pines. There is almost complete freedom from dust, with the exception of the carbon, &c., from the chimneys, which, of course, depends on the number of habitations, and the stillness of the air.

Taken as a whole, these conditions are healthy and exhilarating, and the mental effect of the sunlight on many patients who have been habitually spending much of their time indoors at home, is most cheering and beneficial. The value of exposure to fresh air in many diseases is becoming more widely known and appreciated, and its benefit to phthisical cases, provided they escape attacks of catarrh and bronchitis, &c., cannot be doubted, whilst the tonicity of mountain air in anæmia, debility, dyspepsia, some uterine complaints, &c., and convalescence from acute diseases, are too well known by Anglo-Indians to require repetition.

Therapeutical Effects of Cold.—Cold increases the ap-

(a) For the sun-hours of the Maloja, Davos, Wiesen, St. Moritz, vide page 90.

petite probably from its exhilarating powers, and the requirements in the body of more hydro-carbons to meet a normal increase in combustion. A well-known writer on therapeutics remarks that the most vigorous health is maintained by a rapid construction and destruction of tissue within certain bounds, provided these processes are fairly balanced. Cold, when judiciously applied, is well-known to be a powerful tonic. A cold climate and cold bathing are tonic and bracing. The theory of the tonic action of cold may, perhaps, be stated thus :—During exposure to cold the loss of body-heat, as tested by the thermometer, is by no means the measure of the quantity withdrawn. Many observers have shown that at such times increased combustion occurs, whereby much of the lost heat is compensated, and the temperature is maintained as soon as restored. This increased oxidation of tissue is demonstrated by the greatly increased quantity of carbonic acid thrown off by the lungs on exposure to cold (Ringer). Moderate cold may also be considered a nervine tonic, as it stimulates the nervous system, abolishing that languor and want of energy that heat produces; the most striking example being the "plunge" or "cold douche" after a Turkish bath, and also the capacity for exertion that one possesses in a cold climate. With regard to sanguification, a low temperature causes the lungs to absorb more oxygen, and by thus inducing quicker change in the blood corpuscles, exerts a highly beneficial influence on anæmia.

It has been noticed that many patients have lost their night sweats and high temperatures in the Alps—sometimes after a few days' residence. It is not unlikely that the lower temperature of the surrounding medium, viz., the atmosphere, influences this to some extent, and also, in the case of perspiration, that its stimulating properties brace up the coats of the cutaneous vessels and promote a healthy action of the skin and sudoriparous glands. Some analogy appears to exist between the action of cold on temperature, and the effects of quinine and salicylic acid : these agents often reduce a high temperature, but have a markedly diminished action on the normal heat of the body.

Moderate cold appears to influence the desire, as well as the capability, for movement and exercise ; thereby maintaining the body in working order or training deficient organs up to a state of physiological activity by the stir which Nature urges, for the comfort, satisfaction, or warmth of the individual. It can be readily understood that the employment of the various organs and limbs of the human frame is essential to their efficiency. From disuse, man has lost the grasping power of the foot, and the toes of the present species are atrophied, although the tendons remain. It becomes a question to be considered whether the sedentary occupations of modern civilisation will not eventually favour a pseudo-atrophy of organs connected with the respiratory and circulatory systems. How many men, dwellers in any of the large cities, having reached the term of years generally styled the "prime of life," could run a hundred yards with comfort, or mount a staircase rapidly without breathlessness or palpitation? With women the case is even worse, an additional curb being placed on the act of respiration by modern listlessness and fashionable attire.

The value of cold high climates in pulmonary complaints is, in a great measure, the consequence of a gentle training of the respiratory functions, the lungs becoming expanded without calling for the usual stimulus of muscular effort, which in many conditions of disease would be injurious or perhaps dangerous from the consequent force given to the pulmonary circulation.

Rattray has made observations on the weight and height of forty-eight naval cadets, aged from $14\frac{1}{2}$ to 17 years, during four successive changes of climate during a voyage. The results show that in the Tropics they increased in height more rapidly than in cold climates, but that they lost weight very considerably and, in spite of their rapid growth, Rattray concludes that the heat impaired the strength, weight, and health of these lads. His figures seem conclusive on these points, and show the beneficial influence of cold on youths belonging to races long resident in temperate climates. (Parkes' "Hygiene," p. 436.)

Sunlight.—That light has an action on the blood corpuscles may be easily proved by observing the large number of workers in mines and dark factories, shop girls, clerks, &c., who suffer from anæmia; likewise stokers on board ship and sailors employed entirely between decks or in the hold of a vessel, where the amount of light is necessarily limited, or perhaps entirely absent; these men, if contrasted with the workers on the upper deck, compare unfavourably in healthy appearances, although as regards diet and sea-air, some of them are very nearly under the same conditions. Referring to Arctic experiences, there is every reason to expect the converse of the depressing influence exercised by the prolonged and intense darkness of the Arctic night.

Dr. W. Hammond contributed a paper in the "Medico-Chirurgical Transactions," on the influence of light, showing that the development of tadpoles may be retarded by depriving them of light; and that in an experiment with two kittens, where one was confined in a dark box and the other in a box to which light was admitted, the weight was perceptibly increased by light, while the growth of the other was retarded. Various experiments demonstrate that the action of light is of benefit in many conditions, anæmia, chlorosis, and phthisis being among the number. Other factors enter largely into the cause of anæmia, &c., but the want of sunlight bears on it very strongly. The aspect of health which is created by the sun's rays speaks for itself, showing that light is a therapeutic agent of much value.

The chemical action in plants depends greatly on the presence of sunlight with the chlorophyl. Some gases also which do not combine in darkness, immediately do so on exposure to strong light.

Barometric Pressure.—In approaching the subject of barometric pressure, it will be interesting to first quote the experiences of Glaisher, Gay Lussac, and others, of its result on the action of the pulse and respiration.

Balloon ascents of	Feet.	Increase in pulse.
Biot and Gay Lussac	9,000	18 to 30
Glaisher	17,000	10 to 24
	24,000	24 to 31

An ascent by Glaisher and Coxwell on the 17th July 1862, gave these results:

Mr. Glaisher's pulse	76
Mr. Coxwell's pulse	74
At 17,000 feet, Glaisher	100
„ „ Coxwell	84

21st August at 1,000 feet.	At 11,000.
Mr. Coxwell . . 95	90
Mr. Ingelow . . 80	100
Captain Percival . 90	88

The humidity of the air was found to decrease with the height in a wonderfully decreasing ratio, till at heights exceeding five miles the amount of aqueous vapour in the atmosphere was found to be very small indeed. (a)

The number of pulsations usually increased with elevation, as also the number of respirations. (b)

Arnieux, in the case of eighty-six invalids removed from the plains to Barèges at a height of 4,000 feet, satisfied himself, after a residence of four months, the respirations were

---

(a) "Lectures in Exeter Hall," by Glaisher.
(b) Glaisher's "Travels in the Air," 1871.

increased by two, and the beats of the pulse reduced by four. He had also found on careful examination that the eighty-six men had in four months gained on an average one inch in girth round the chest.

Dr. Kellett found that the invalids at Landour gained one inch, chiefly during the first two weeks. (a)

Jourdanet has asserted (" Du Mexique," page 76) that the usual notion that the respirations are augmented in number in the inhabitants of high lands is "completely erroneous; that the respirations are, in fact, lessened; and that from time to time a deeper inspiration is involuntarily made as partial compensation."

But Coindet from 1,500 observations on French and Mexicans does not confirm this. The mean number of respirations was—

19·36 per minute for the French,
20·297   „   „   Mexicans.

(PARKES.)

From these and more recent observations, evidence is in favour of a slight increase both in the pulse and respirations in persons first dwelling at high altitudes, but the length of time these phenomena last has not been noted with much accuracy. It must not be forgotten, however, that the increase in the measurements of the chest, and the excursions forward of the sternum, after a short residence in Alpine valleys, may also in a great measure be explained by the gain in flesh and strength, for we know that on convalescence from many diseases at *low* altitudes this event is a consequence of returning health, and a token of general improvement.

Oxygen.—The difference in the amount of oxygen inhaled at an ascent of 6,000 feet is as follows :—

In a cubic foot of dry air at 32° Fah., and 30 inches

(a) "M. R.," vol. lviii., 1876.

barometric pressure, we find 130,375 grains of oxygen. A man draws on an average when tranquil 16·6 cubic feet of air into his lungs per hour, $130{\cdot}375 \times 16{\cdot}6 = 2164{\cdot}2$ grains of oxygen (Parkes). An ascent (about 6,000 feet) where the barometer stands at 24 inches, will reduce this 1-5th, or $\left(\frac{24 \times 130\cdot4}{30}\right) = 1043{\cdot}2$ grains, lessening the quantity per hour by 432·4 grains.

Without allowing for a slight difference of oxygen at high altitudes, owing to the small amount of moisture in the air, about four additional respirations per minute would be necessary to compensate for a barometric fall of six inches, but by experiments on animals it has been found that as long as the percentage of oxygen was not below 14, the same quantity was absorbed into the blood as when the gas was in normal proportion. The quantity of oxygen in the atmosphere surrounding animals appears to have very little influence on the amount of this gas absorbed by them, for the quantity consumed is not greater, even though an excess of oxygen be added to the atmosphere experimented with (Regnault and Reiset). It therefore does not seem at all probable that the lessened *weight* of oxygen taken into the lungs, when breathing rarefied air at 6,000 feet, necessitates any increase in the number of respirations. This is not unworthy of notice when we reflect that in phthisis and some forms of anæmia there is diminished respiratory function.

The explanation why breathing mountain air should increase the number of respirations and expand the lungs cannot be satisfactorily accounted for by the laws of mechanical pressure, as the diminution is everywhere the same, both internally and externally, and such an equilibrium of force being established disposes of any theory which attributes increased thoracic capacity, directly to diminished barometric pressure.

The rhythm of the involuntary movements of the chest-walls and diaphragm depend entirely on nervous influence, and it would appear that the cause of extended respiratory movements depends on the excitation of the respiratory centres, influenced, amongst other causes, by certain fibres which run in the course of the pneumogastric. Rarefied air irritating these fibres would therefore account for the additional number of respirations and extended chest-movements. An increased proportion of blood in the lungs would also tend to this result.

In the cold high altitudes we may, then, attribute the change to both these causes, but whether this phenomenon occurs in persons whose lungs are already quickened in action by disease is a matter for observation. In these cases the exciting cause of respiratory rhythm depends more on the proportion of carbonic acid and oxygen in the blood than on the density of the air breathed.

The following facts prove that this condition of the blood influences the respiratory movements:— 1. The respiratory movements can be totally arrested if, either by a forced artificial respiration (by blowing air into the lungs) or by forced voluntary breathing, the blood becomes saturated with oxygen and poor in carbonic acid ("apnœa"). 2. Respiration becomes stronger, and the more accessory muscles take part in it ("dyspnœa"). The poorer in oxygen and the richer in carbonic acid the blood is, as, *e.g.*, on the entrance of air or fluid into the pleural cavities, causing a collapse of the lung, or when, by inflammation, &c., the lungs are unfit for respiration (Hermann's "Physiology").

There are three causes at high altitudes which advance the combination of the carbon and hydrogen of the body with the oxygen of the air, viz., cold air, sunlight, and lessened pressure; therefore, it is conceivable that the additional weight of oxygen absorbed by the blood does not become such an overplus as would, when reaching the medulla, induce a tendency to apnœa, but may be sufficient to exert some inhibitory influence and balance irritation of the peripheral fibres of the pneumograstic in the lungs. Or, to summarise thus:

1. Rarefied air and larger proportion of blood in the lungs, increasing respiration.

2. Oxygen in blood circulating to medulla, retarding respiration.

The balance being a little in favour of No. 1 in healthy persons; but in impaired lungs with quickened action (owing to excess of carbonic acid in the blood) the increased quantity of oxygen absorbed by the blood at high levels seems to have a proportionately stronger inhibitory influence. This appears to be borne out by the fact of many patients breathing comparatively freely when leaving the plains who again experience dyspnœa on their return from the mountains.

From the experiments of Dr. Marcet at high altitudes in Switzerland and the Island of Teneriffe, it appears that more air in bulk, but less in weight, is breathed at high altitudes, and that a larger proportion of carbonic acid is excreted in the cold altitudes of Switzerland (showing that more oxygen has been absorbed).

At Teneriffe the carbonic acid was not increased in amount, whereas in the Swiss altitudes of 13,000 feet an increase of 15 per cent. was discovered. We can attribute this to the lower temperature of the latter country (as Dr. Marcet observed), and also to the larger amount of sunlight, and in a *cold* high climate there would be a greater volume of blood in the lungs to avail itself of the absorption of the oxygen.

One may be said to live quickly at these altitudes, and the most perfect health is maintained by a rapid waste and repair of the tissues of the body. This increased combustion does not mean shortened existence, but improved health, provided that repair and loss are equally balanced.

Theoretically, lungs which would be incapable of performing the respiratory functions completely at sea-level would, on the patient rising to higher cold levels, utilise more oxygen in proportion to the weight of the air inhaled the higher they ascend, within ordinary limits, and that the functions of the skin would also be promoted by reduced pressure, favouring the action of osmosis. (*a*)

Although, perhaps, not quite so much fresh air is breathed in a cold climate by those who sleep with closed windows as is breathed in the warmer health resorts by persons who sleep with the windows open, the three conditions of excessive sunlight, cold atmosphere, and lessened barometric pressure, may partly compensate for the advantage in that respect. Indeed, it is difficult everywhere to persuade many patients to ventilate their rooms at night.

Before leaving this subject, it will be interesting to note the diminution of barometric pressure, in the Engadine, viz., 677,476 lbs. of the whole of the human body. Although the considerable reduction of three tons (*b*) taken off the fluids, and solid parts of the skeleton carries with it no remarkable phenomenon, it is not illogical to assume that such a declension in the weight of the atmosphere must exert some peculiar powers. Whether these affect physiological actions, or influence the animal economy in any way other than favouring the interchange of gases; increasing the beats of the pulse and the number of respirations; rendering

---

(*a*) There is evidence that the interchange of gases between the air and the blood through the skin has an important share in keeping up the temperature of the body, and we find the temperature of the surface much elevated in cases of pneumonia, phthisis, &c., in which the lungs seem to perform their function very insufficiently (Carpenter's "Human Physiology").

(*b*) The barometer is lowered about 6 inches, 1/5th of the capacity of the mercurial column at sea-level. A cubic inch of mercury weighs 3,433·5 grains, or ·49 lb. The surface of an ordinary sized man is about 16 square feet; therefore the calculation can be easily made.

muscular exertion less fatiguing; may be elucidated by future observations.

Ozone.—This peculiar condition of oxygen is generally found in healthy localities. Sea-air and mountainous tracts especially give indications of its presence, whilst in densely populated districts or unhealthy places, ozone is observed only in small quantities. In a work on "Ozone and Antozone" Dr. Cornelius Fox states as follows:—"The salubrity of a town or city may be pretty accurately estimated by the effects of its air on ozonoscopes, as the feebleness and sluggishness of the re-action is a very good gauge of the amount of impurities which it contains. Ozone is a deodorising and purifying agent of the highest order, resolving and decomposing into innocuous forms. The oils of the cod's liver, the cocoa-nut, and sun-flower, *when ozonised*, have been found, by Drs. Theophilus and Symes Thompson, to be very useful in reducing the rapidity of the pulse, and exerting at the same time an invigorating influence on the heart's action in consumption. Last in order, but first in importance, ozone has been considered to be probably concerned in a work most gigantic in magnitude and of vital consequence. It has been thought to be influential in the modification of climate, to exercise a beneficial action on animal and vegetable life, and to be indispensable to the relief and cure of functional disorder and disease. It has been doubted whether life could continue to exist on this planet, according to the present constitution of terrestrial laws, if the formation of ozone should cease in nature."

It is, perhaps, too soon to say that ozone is obnoxious to micro-organisms, nevertheless, the latter diminish with increase of ozone. In the elevated Alps, where there is constantly recurring atmospheric states of electrical high tension, large quantities of air become ozonised, and it is in these regions that micro-organisms have been found by Pasteur, Miquel, Tyndall, and others, to be greatly diminished in numbers and at some heights, as for instance on the Aletsch glacier, at an altitude of 2,300 mètres, Tyndall found that sterilised infusions were unaltered when the flasks when opened and closed again ; but, in a hay-loft, twenty-one flasks out of twenty-three showed living organisms, when manipulated in the same manner.

The researches of M. le Professeur Yung, of Geneva, and Edouard de Freudenreich, of Bern, carry with them some valuable evidences of the purity of mountain air, in comparison with that of the plains. M. de Freudenreich has evidently devoted much time to these important investigations. In the summer of last year many delicate experiments were made by him at the Col de St. Théodule (3,322 mètres), Aletsch glacier, Niesen (2,366 mètre), Lake of Thun, &c.

The methods of procedure were similar to those originated by Miquel, of Paris, the director of the Montsouris Observatory. M. de Freudenreich after demonstrating the entire absence of germs in the quantity of air examined (300 to 1,500 litres), at such altitudes as the Eiger (3,975 m.). The foot of the Eiger (2,100 m.). The Strahlegg and the Schilthorn, attributes the diminution in the number of microbes in the high regions, to the following causes :—

1. To the progressive disappearance of productive foci for bacteria, according to height, until the zone of eternal snow is reached, when the disappearance of these foci are absolute.

2. To the lessening density of the atmosphere, which becomes less able to hold microscopic particles in suspension : at the same time a diminution of dust from the same and other causes.

In an interesting *brochure* on "Living Organisms of the Air," he also mentions the recent researches of M. le Commandant Moreau, published in the *Semaine Medicale*, of 6th March, 1884, by Dr. Miquel. These researches show that only five or six bacteria were found by Moreau, in sea-air.

Now, there can be little doubt from these and other observations that the relation of micro-organisms to ozone is in an inverse ratio: for on the sea and in mountain air where ozone abounds, microbes diminish. Although temperature, a thin atmosphere, and absence of productive forci clearly affect the development of micro-organisms, the power exerted in this direction by an ozoniferous atmosphere is well worthy of careful investigation.

CHAPTER III.

"Cold" as a Sensation and as Temperature.—Characteristics of Alpine Climate, and its Effects on the Vascularity of the Lungs and on Nutrition.

THOSE who are unacquainted with high altitudes in winter may perhaps be inclined to judge the sensations at a high cold region from an English standard of cold, thinking possibly that twenty degrees of frost signifies twenty degrees of chilliness, and that any temperature below freezing point would be likely to cause discomfort to delicate persons. A brief explanation may tend to correct this view. The body can be deprived of its heat in four different ways :—

1. By conduction, or contact with colder substances, either solid, fluid, or gaseous.

2. By evaporation from the surface of the skin, and the mucous membrane of the respiratory tract.

3. By excretory matters leaving the body ; and

4. By radiation.

Now, although it is possible from the hygrometric state of the atmosphere that an additional quantity of moisture is evaporated from the skin and respiratory tract, at high levels,(a) this variation plays a very minor part in sensibly

---

(a) It must not be supposed that evaporation from the body depends entirely on the percentage of humidity in the air. The conservative and balancing agencies of physiological action amongst other things constringe or dilate the cutaneous capillaries in response to cold or heat, rest or exertion, &c.

reducing the temperature of the body compared to the abstraction of heat by conduction; or, in other words, contact with cold air in movement. This latter cause is the one which principally bears on the question of sensation, inasmuch as cause No. 3 is too insignificant to be felt, and No. 4 can be guarded against to a great extent by clothing.

The physical sensibility of cold is produced by the amount of heat rather suddenly abstracted from the body (which does not always depend on the temperature in contact with it). For example, if the hand be placed on fur at 30° Fahr., it feels warm in comparison with iron at the same temperature. The former being a bad conductor—owing to the *motionless* air in its interstices—does not abstract much heat from the hand; the metal, being a good conductor of heat, appears intensely cold to the touch.

If, therefore, cold-motionless-dry air surrounds the body, heat is not abstracted nearly so readily as it would be by somewhat warmer air in movement. It must be remembered that the sensation of cold cannot be accurately gauged by reference to the thermometer. Two other conditions are intimately connected with temperature in causing impressions of cold or heat—viz., wind and moisture, for it is these that cool the body, by conduction. If their temperature is lower than ours, they appear colder than they really are, because from their conductivity heat quickly passes away from us.

In the high valleys of the Alps, although the thermometer may register some 15° or 20° of frost, this low temperature is by no means disagreeable, as the calm air and intense solar heat enable many persons to sit in the open and bask in the sun during the depth of winter without feeling the slightest sensation of chilliness. Even excessive tanning and reddening of the skin takes place with almost everyone who takes plenty of outdoor exercise: ladies, who are generally well protected by sunshades or umbrellas, do not escape a healthful aspect. This is mostly owing to the reflection of light from the snow, which coming in upward and parallel directions, cannot be well screened from the face. The habit and necessity of wearing smoked-glass spectacles also enables persons to face the glare, and thereby receive a much larger proportion of light than in England. (*a*) According to Dr. Cornelius Fox, ozone also causes a healthy colouration of exposed parts of the body. The speedy tanning that one undergoes when crossing a mountain pass, or driving in an open sleigh, supports this view. As more ozone is brought into contact with the skin by movement through air when driving, or on the passes where there is generally a breeze present, so a greater colouration ensues; whereas one may be exposed to the influence of wind in large cities (where there is an absence or great diminution of ozone) without wearing a rosy or tanned appearance.

The general climatic characteristics are—

1. Dryness of the air (*b*) and its comparative freedom from micro-organisms, mechanical irritants, and noxious gases.

(*a*) It has been frequently noticed that dark-complexioned individuals become sunburnt more readily than "blondes." This depends principally on the sensitiveness of the retina and the colour of the eyes. For instance, "fair" people cannot face the light with such ease and comfort as those who have plenty of pigment in their ires; for the pigment absorbing the rays of light, protects the retina, and even enables some with very "dark" eyes, to gaze on the sun itself. On the other hand, a person with a grey or pale iris averts and screens the eyes from the sunlight as much as possible, and in this way escapes the effect of the rays on the face.

(*b*) The drying and preserving of meat hung in the air, has been alluded to as an illustration of the dryness of these climates. This takes place in an analogous manner to the drying of turtle in the sun in the West Indies, viz., evaporation of moisture before putrefaction takes place. In the Swiss mountains the vitality of germs being rendered inert by a low temperature, thick masses of meat can be gradually dried.

2. Low temperature.
3. Profusion of sunlight.
4. Diminished barometric pressure.
5. Ozoniferous atmosphere.

The results on pulmonary complaints, anæmia, and allied disorders, may be stated thus :—

1. By breathing aseptic air free from dust, irritation or perhaps, recurrence of infection by microbes in the respiratory tract, is greatly lessened.
2. Vaporisation of morbid secretions in the lungs takes place, promoted by reduced barometric pressure and dryness of the atmosphere.
3. Increased oxidation of blood and tissue, from sunlight, cold air, and reduced pressure.
4. Increased quantity of blood circulating in the lungs— caused by the low temperature—the freedom of the circulation being aided by extended chest movements.
5. Increased activity in the pulmonary lymphatics (depending on circulation and expansion) and a general improvement in nutrition and glandular secretion; also an exhilarating effect on the nervous system.

Some of these results are obtainable under no other conditions than those presented at high cold regions. With regard to the increased quantity of blood circulating in the lungs (presumably influencing the nutrition of those organs), it may be contended that this is not a desirable sequence. Perhaps it is not in hæmorrhagic phthisis; but in some other forms, especially early tubercular deposits, it would not seem to be disadvantageous. What would lead one to suppose this, is the rare occurrence of tubercular phthisis in persons affected with mitral disease. Even when hæmoptysis takes place, and when some of the blood presumably gravitates into the air cells, tubercular disease rarely follows; whilst, on the other hand, phthisis is not an uncommon consequence after hæmoptysis from other causes. This would appear to indicate that a general hyperæmic condition of the lungs impedes the deposition of tubercle and restrains phthisical processes. Support is also lent to this view by tubercle generally attacking the apices of the lungs, which parts contain rather less blood, owing to gravitation.

Conversely, where the quantity of blood circulating in the lungs is diminished, as in hot climates, phthisis is frequently seen to run a very rapid course.

It is not improbable that this increased volume of blood moving in an impaired and imperfect lung at a high altitude plays an important part in the nutrition of the tissues and in augmenting the movement of lymph through the pulmonary lymphatics, so removing by absorption many of the smaller morbid cell growths. With the lessened barometric pressure accelerating the action of osmosis, compensation to some extent is made for the loss in pulmonary capacity, for we know that a more rapid interchange of gases takes place under reduced pressure.

On the other hand, the emphysematous signs presented by patients who may be said to be cured, after a prolonged residence at high stations, may seem to contra-indicate any theory based on this assumption. It must be conceded, however, that with the expansion of the chest obtained, it is doubtful if emphysema occasions such compression of the pulmonary capillaries as to decrease the *whole* volume of blood circulating in the lungs.

That the lungs contain more blood in a cold climate is pretty clear, if we accept the evidence of Dr. Francis (Bengal Army), who found from a large number of observations, that the lungs are lighter after death in Europeans in India than the European standard. Parkes confirms this, and also Rattray, in his observations of diminished respiratory function in hot climates.

When the activity of any organ of the body is augmented,

more blood is attracted to it than when at rest, or during lessened exertion. By breathing rarefied air at high levels the respiratory movements are usually quickened and extended, especially on taking exercise.

The liability, also, of the natives of these high valleys to pneumonia, whilst exempt from phthisis, would seem to point to some alteration in the vascular condition of the organs affected. What result any variation in the vascularity of the lungs would have on the bacillus tuberculosis is rather premature to surmise. No bacilli have, however, up to the present time been discovered in the blood of tubercular subjects. It appears, therefore, that either they do not enter the vessels in the form of a bacillus, or if entering, are changed in character or destroyed. That the state of the blood, chemical or pathological condition, or functional activity of the tissues must be agencies governing the suitability of the soil for the reception of a bacillus, is supported by the fact that infection is very rare, although there are numberless cases in which bacilli have undoubtedly been inhaled.

There is, however, no decided criterion for the determination of the question whether—

1. A major quantity of blood in the lungs, such as may be diffused through these organs in a high cold climate, with slightly augmented freedom (from acceleration of respiratory and cardiac movements) and more complete oxidation, is or is not less disposed to bring about pulmonary hæmorrhage than—

2. A minor proportion of blood at sea-level, circulating with less facility, and not so effectually oxidised.

The problem also appears to present itself as one of "nutrition of the lung," viz., whether slight hyperæmia (under those circumstances) is not a more desirable sequence than the inclination to slight blood stasis of No. 2.

It is well known, also, that the hygrometric and barometric states of the atmosphere modify the process of evaporation from the lungs and skin. The evaporation of morbid secretions in the lungs was pointed out in 1881 (a) as being one of the circumstances which probably has an important bearing on phthisis. The process of evaporation in dry climates, acting on ulcers, cavities, or suppurating surfaces, if not analogous to the dry treatment of wounds (so successfully carried out by Mr. Gamgee, of Birmingham), brings about a less moist and watery condition of the secretions from diseased bronchial tubes or cavities of the lung; virtually imitating expectoration without the patient undergoing the effort of coughing.

The effects on the body of sunlight and reduced pressure are doubtless those facilitating the interchange of gases in the blood and tissues, whilst the cold air necessitates the requirement of a larger absorption of oxygen and assimilation of hydro-carbons to maintain the heat of the body. It may be conjectured that this contributes to the sudden and considerable push given to nutrition on arrival at a cold high altitude, when the appetite is, in most cases, at once improved in a remarkable way, and animal food that could hardly be thought of previously without disgust is eaten promptly. Where improvement begins it is difficult to say; indeed it is only to a combination of causes that the variety of effects can be attributed. This push to nutrition is a reliable feature in the first evidences of progression, and assures a certain amount of hopefulness in the case.

The exhilarating feeling produced by the *consciousness* of moving about amid snow and ice, without taking cold or feeling pinched, is not to be despised as contributing towards cure. The contrast of this with the life in England during winter, where every change of weather has to be guarded

---

(a) "Davos Platz, and the Effects of Altitude on Phthisis."—(*The Author.*)

against, is so marked that the hope of recovery presents itself, and despondency is banished.

There is every reason to suppose that under the many favourable circumstances presented by these climates the treatment of suitable cases of anæmia and its allies, scrofula, consumption, and affections of the chest, and some cachectic states of the system, can be undertaken with greater confidence, and those measures which have of late years prolonged many valuable lives, are certainly more likely to be efficient and successful, when supported by the curative effects of mountain air; whilst for the somewhat minor maladies, such as debility, either from physical causes, or from mental fatigue and worry, malaria, &c., some forms of dyspepsia, chronic discharges or suppurations (that do not incapacitate the patient from taking gentle exercise), and during convalescence from many acute diseases, the renovating power of these remarkable climates are, in suitable cases, doubtless far superior in rapidity of effect, to warmer and lower latitudes.

It is not for a moment implied that climatic conditions, grateful at all times in health and disease, are not found in certain localities, where the range of the thermometer is generally from $50°$ to $65°$, or thereabouts. This equality of temperature with dryness, &c., enables patients to be constantly in the open air, and if not out of the house, to be able to avail themselves of a system of "hyperventilation" day and night; but, on the other hand, it is now well known that other places can be found as favourable, if not more so, for these complaints in cold climates, although the range of the temperature is not so limited; whilst the languor and depression of strength felt in warm climates is altogether escaped.

COIRE.

CHAPTER IV.

Including the Drawbacks of the Alpine Winter Stations.

AFTER leaving Coire (a) for the ascent to Churwalden (4,976 ft.) and Parpan (4,938 ft.) the beauties of the mountain journey begin. The rise in the altitude gives a sensation of lightness and elasticity to the frame. All the surroundings cheer the spirits—the tinkling music of the cow-bells, the autumnal changes in foliage, golden larches and aspens contrasting with the dark green of the firs, topped here and there by brilliant sun-beams, undulating into gorges and hollows of obscure impenetrable shades—whilst in the distance are occasionally seen the higher peaks crowned with dazzling snow of snowy whiteness. After a railway journey perhaps from foggy London, these scenes alone stimulate and recruit the strength. It is well to be cautious at this stage, that the powers are not overtaxed by fatigue ; for this sudden vigour is not yet permanent, but may permit a delicate person unconsciously to out-run the supply of force. It is, in some instances, desirable that the journey from London for example, should be broken at various points, so that the patient shall not reach his destination in a wearied and jaded state.

The transformation scene after the winter snow has

(a) Davos Platz and Davos Dörfli can be reached from Landquart, the station before Chûr (*vide* page 16).

fallen intensifies all the virtues of mountain air. With the sudden covering of the earth by a non-conducting material an entirely new condition of the climate is established. Fresh breezes have died away, packs of cumulus cloud have been condensed into snow, the moisture in the atmosphere is of the smallest quantity, whilst the sun shines with the lustre and power of the South, and the sky presents an almost unclouded surface of azure blue.

There are, however, many cases of advanced disease buoyed up with false hopes, in real ignorance of their true condition, who, instead of seeking the soothing and languid influences of a Southern clime, or the comforts of home, venture to face suddenly the stimulating and force-producing powers of the keen mountain air. To countenance the reception of unsuitable cases with the chance of recovery that occasionally presents itself in pulmonary disease, is not only reprehensible and bad, but detracts from the value of "climate" as a remedy of even limited application. We cannot but think that this is one of the reasons which has somewhat retarded the frank reception by the medical faculty of Alpine regions, as offering a means of cure to many who can arrange to spend the winter amidst the snow and sunlight of the Swiss mountains.

The great drawback to some of these health-resorts, as with many others in the South, is defective sanitation. As long as overcrowding does not take place, the cold and snow will, to a great extent, mitigate the evils of bad drainage and impure emanations; but when hotels get filled with a large number of visitors, many of whom may be in delicate health, the air within will not (except by artificial ventilation and good house drainage) be free from the usual indoor impurities, as sewer-gas, kitchen and basement air, exhalations from the lungs and skin of organic matter, scales of epithelium, fibres of cotton, wool, wood, &c., the products of combustion from gas, lamps, and candles; bacteria and fungi; and, what is, perhaps, more important still in the case of delicate lungs bacilli floating about in the air. Patients must, therefore exercise their own discretion in opening windows and airing their rooms as much as possible. During fine weather a fair quantity of fresh air can always be permitted to enter the bed-rooms, according to the desire of the individual; but in other parts of the houses the means of admitting pure air and providing for the escape of foul are very imperfect. Until appliances are introduced into the hotels (as is done in the Maloja Kursaal) to clean the air, warm, moisten, and medicate it if necessary, every high altitude station can scarcely be designated "air-cure place," for most of the patient's time is spent indoors, where the conditions in some of the hotels are no better than at home—perhaps worse, if the house should be full of people, "The breath of even healthy persons often contained microbes, and the moisture in the breath, if collected, was putrescible, and when condensed upon the walls of an apartment or elsewhere, doubtless formed productive *foci* for micro-organisms."—(G. V. Poore, M.D., Cantor Lectures.)

By boxing-up soiled air for the sake of warmth, the pollution of the interior of dwellings by organic matter can be readily discerned by anyone who is familiar with its peculiar odour. In crowded places of entertainment, on first entering from the outside, a faint, musty smell is not uncommon. This indicates an atmosphere loaded with organic impurities, and the immediate effects of such commence with faintness and headache. The quantity of carbonic acid evolved is in no sense so dangerous as the animal matter, although it gives a good clue in estimating the quantity of the latter poison.

Where stoves are in use, attention should be given to them to see that servants do not entirely close the valve which regulates the flue. Occasionally this is done, when the fuel is consumed and the remains are glowing red, with the intention of economising heat, which it effectually does, by preventing air passing through and cooling the stove; but the most poisonous of all gases, viz., carbonic oxide, is slowly evolved into the room from the dying embers and quickly gives rise to headache, which is not rapidly shaken off even by fresh air. (*a*)

It is essential, too, that some special employment should be undertaken when persons remain several months abroad; languages can be studied, or the mind occupied with work of some sort. By this means time does not drag heavily, *ennui* is not experienced, and restoration to health is not retarded by dejection of spirits.

The travelling also has to be considered. Those who are in pretty fair health can make the journey in three days, either to Maloja, St. Moritz, Davos, or Wiesen, but a longer time is recommended for those whose health does not admit of prolonged confinement in railway carriages. The journey may be broken at Paris or Brussels, Bâle, and Chûr, Como, or Promontogno, according to the route chosen by the traveller.

On first arrival it occasionally happens with some people that they are unable to obtain a good night's rest for the first night or so. This depends on the sudden rise which they have made to high regions. The difficulty soon passes off; but in the case of sensitive persons who sleep badly, it may be met by remaining a few days at Chûr (1,936 ft.). The stay there will frequently help in training the system to the new conditions. It must not be forgotten that the altered form of bed may, in many instances, prevent sound and refreshing sleep. The wedge-shaped hair bolster can sometimes be removed with great advantage to the sleeper, and extra clothing be placed over the shoulders and upper part of

(*a*) Carbonic oxide replaces oxygen in the blood, and cannot be again replaced by oxygen, but has to be slowly converted into carbonic acid, before elimination.

the body which is usually not covered by the eider-down quilt. In addition to equalising the bed temperature in this way, the head should not be raised at too great an angle from the chest and shoulders, or compression of the vessels of the neck will ensue, and so impede the ready return of blood from the brain, keeping this organ active and full, when it should be in the anæmic state which usually accompanies sleep.

A little discomfort is sometimes caused by chilblains during the winter time. To prevent these, walking exercise should be taken immediately after breakfast, and the endeavour be made to keep the feet warm throughout the day by this means. The parquet floors, although healthy and advantageous in many respects, are, in a great measure, the cause of cold feet and the source of chilblains, therefore all the corridors and bed-rooms in hotels should be carpeted in these climates during winter time.

What has been advanced as an objection to Alpine stations is the use of the German stove as a means of warming the interior of houses and hotels. The fault, however, does not lie so much with the ponderous German *Ofen* as with improper management in neglecting to provide sufficient ventilation for the rooms and moisture for the air. An improvement on these stoves is the steam reservoirs in use at the Kurhaus, Davos Platz, the admission of steam being under the control of the occupant of the room in which they are placed. But this plan also raises the temperature without raising the "dew-point," or, in popular language, "dries the air," creating a necessity for a supply of watery vapour to render the atmosphere fit for healthy and agreeable respiration; for, although dryness of the climate is one of the main features of the Swiss Alps, a limit can be reached beyond which a dessicating effect may be produced.

The introduction to the bright and calm winters of these

regions is sometimes a little unsettled, but not dangerously so. Falls of snow occur and are apt to thaw again; the roads, however, soon dry, by reason of the sloping land and rapid evaporation. Acclimatisation has frequently been held up as a pre-requisite for visitors, but, as the winter is generally bright, calm, with dry cold and plenty of sun, the risk of arrival, even after the commencement of winter, is in no wise greater than during the autumn. To become acclimatised for one of the best seasons of the year, and one which is regarded as a "cure" period, requires no inurement —many persons even arriving in mid-winter and crossing a mountain pass without inconvenience or harm resulting. The selection of an Alpine station should certainly be influenced by the opinion of physicians at home, even where the intention is entertained of returning for a second or third winter. Perhaps this may seem to be written in the interests of the medical profession, but those who have spent three or four seasons at these places will have observed that some cases return again who would do better in a southern clime. An over-estimation of their own recuperative powers, or an enthusiastic belief in the potency of the charming Alpine climate to sweep away *all* maladies, is possibly the cause of an injudicious decision.

Children over three years of age do extremely well in the Alps, make healthy blood and muscle, gain flesh, and expand their chests. Under this age, it is doubtful if sufficient exercise can be taken by a child to ward off the cold, without being swathed to such an extent in furs and flannels as would impede the free motions of the limbs and thorax, so essential to development in childhood.

It is also a moot question whether some invalids should not quit the Alps immediately the end of the winter seems approaching, as the changeable weather, with wet roads, winds, &c., is likely to upset many of the benefits gained during the dry season. In this case, it would probably be well to go south, Lugano (982 ft.), Como (705 ft.), Sorrento &c.; but if spring has set in, the shores of Lac Léman (1,230 ft.) offer a fairly safe change. Thusis (2,448 ft.), has attracted many persons from Davos, it is a pretty place, with agreeable walks and fairly comfortable hotels. Ragatz (1,709 ft.), Mels (1,637 ft.) are reached easily, but a residence at these latter has seldom been attended with much improvement in health. Promontogno (2,700 ft.) is very convenient for the Engadine; its position and climate go a great way in recommending it as a halting-place: measures are being taken by the proprietor of the hotel there to warm the rooms and corridors, as it is well-known that much depends on the comfort and equable temperature within doors during springtime. Coire (1,900 ft.) according to Dr. Killias shows a dry climate in the spring. This town, for some reason or another, has been overlooked, although it has many recommendations as a half-way station.

		Station.	Barometric Height.	Mean Temperature.	Mean Cloudiness.	Rainfall in Millemètres.
					per cent.	
1872 to 1875	March, April, and May.	Thusis	746ᵐ	9.11	56	214.9
		Chür	603ᵐ	9.27	63	149.7
		Ragatz	541ᵐ	9.22	44	335.9

A month might be spent at any of these, previous to returning home, provided the weather is fine, but it is well to be impressed with the necessity of the great personal care needed during this migratory period, especially with regard to clothing. Thick flannels, socks, &c., should not be dispensed with hastily, and it would be well to guard against the change from the calm regions by adopting outer garments of close texture, impervious to the chilling effects of wind.

Any remarks on the climate of Switzerland would be incomplete without reference being made to the föhn wind. (a)

Altitude and low temperature modify, to some extent, the noxious qualities of the wind.

The föhn is a moist southerly aërial current. Its temperature in Switzerland becomes elevated from various causes, the chief of which is probably atmospheric pressure. By this accession of heat the capability of the föhn for holding more moisture in suspension is at once augmented. The "absolute" humidity may remain the same, but by a rise in temperature the percentage of relative humidity (*i.e.*, humidity in relation to the point of saturation), is considerably reduced, for warm air can contain more watery vapour; therefore, the föhn seizes with avidity on any moisture which is present. The extreme dryness is again advanced by the stoves in use, further raising the temperature to a dessicating point. In this way many bad

---

(a) Dr. Wild says, the föhn as such is known only in the north-eastern valleys of Switzerland, and it is there distinguished by its great heat, and still more by its peculiar dryness before which the snow disappears both by rapid melting and also by that rapid evaporation which has obtained for it the appropriate name of the snow-eater (Schneefresser).

But while the föhn proper is blowing in the valleys of the northeast eating away the snow in winter, or in summer and autumn drying the hay or ripening the grapes, over the south-west of Switzerland a warm and wet wind blows, which precipitates its moisture in a heavy down-pour, and floods the country with rain and melted snow. The distinctly föhn stations named by Dr. Wild are, Glarus, Auen, Altdorf, Engleberg, Schwyz, Chûr, and Klosters.

symptoms are aggravated and vaporisation of organic matter takes place, which is doubtless re-inhaled by the occupants of a room badly ventilated or unprovided with sufficient water near the stoves to bedew the air.

The nervous system of most persons becomes remarkably depressed by this wind; the inclination to undergo exertion is diminished; sleep and digestion are disturbed; the animals, too, seem to suffer—effects which closely resemble those caused by the "Vent d'Espagne," in the Pyrenees (Hermann Weber). Indisposition is usually attributed to this wind at Davos, and in several instances with justice.

After one or two days, sometimes longer, the second phase of the föhn is developed. The thermometer falls and with the cooling process the air is gradually brought below the dew-point, and what a few days before was an exceedingly dry wind, becomes converted into an atmosphere saturated with moisture, which falls as snow or rain, according to the time of the year, and temperature.

The days of invasion by the föhn wind are about equal at Davos and Wiesen. On the Maloja plateau, 1.000 feet higher, this wind is rarely felt, and its noxious qualities are greatly modified by the higher altitude, extended width of the valley, and the proximity of immense glaciers to the S. and S.W.

The teeth are apt to cause some trouble in the Alps, if any disposition to caries be present. A good dental surgeon should be consulted previous to leaving home, and the habit be acquired of breathing through the nose as much as possible, even when taking exercise. The rapid changes in the temperature of the teeth occurring to persons who breathe with the mouth, give rise to a variety of derangements, especially in cold climates. Among the natives of Switzerland the noticeable deterioration of the teeth may probably be due to the consumption of the rough wines of the country, which doubtless contain much acetic acid, caries being very marked in the lake districts.

In conclusion, it may not be superfluous to remind those interested that the high cold regions are not yet proved to be the best for *all* cases. The varieties of chest and other affections and the individual differences of affected persons denote that one general climatic panacea is quite inadmissible, and what may be a suitable climate for one, may prove of very little value to another. Whilst some misconception prevails on these points, cold mountain air will not receive the appreciation it merits. It would be inconsistent to contend that any particular health resort had not its drawbacks. It is misleading to make light of these, and most essential in the recommendation of foreign health-resorts that their disadvantages be clearly stated, as well as the probable benefits likely to accrue to persons visiting these places. Much disappointment is thereby averted, and many, who otherwise would expect impossibilities, do not become discontented. In spite of much misunderstanding and opposition, high altitude treatment is gaining ground with the medical profession, and will, no doubt, some day take its right place in climatic therapeutics. Time is needed for the subject to be well threshed out by advocates and opponents alike.

Doubtless nutritious food and properly ventilated houses in good sanitary condition, are indispensable adjuncts to the pure air of the mountains; in these particulars it would conduce more to the advantage of the various health-stations in the Grisons, and to the appreciation of the migrating public, if the numerous resorts vied with each other in attaining to sanitary perfection, rather than in circulating bad opinions and false reports of neighbouring places, pretending to strangers that the climate of no other locality equals or resembles their own.

CHAPTER V.

Winter Clothing.

THE selection of suitable clothing for an Alpine climate will contribute greatly to health as well as to comfort.

The first advice tendered to ladies who seek restoration to health from lung disease is:—Abandon corsets absolutely, and wear the loosest *ceinture* on the waist. This injunction cannot be emphasised too strongly. One prominent sign of what may be termed "cure" of phthisis, at high altitudes, is the almost invariable expansion of the whole or portions of the chest walls. To impede such a beneficial result is to limit the advantages of breathing mountain air. No one could wittingly be guilty of such an irrational procedure as to curtail the actual physical improvement they travel many miles to secure. Yet usually, whilst the upper regions of the chest are allowed free play, the most mobile section, the diaphragm, is fettered and confined in its movements by an unyielding investment pressing on the abdominal viscera. In this way an opposite conformation is maintained against what physiology and common sense would indicate; for in many instances where damage exists in the superior thoracic regions, limitation of movement is desirable in *these* situations, rather than in the lower and sounder parts of the lung.

The substitute for corsets should be a thick flannel

waistcoat or jersey. Flannel should also be worn next the skin over the trunk and extremities. Chamois leather may be substituted when over-sensitiveness of the skin renders the use of flannel unbearable; generally, however, a fine texture can be procured which is not too irritating. A good stock should be taken, as frequent changes are beneficial.

The coverings for the feet and legs require attention. In all cases woollen socks or stockings are indispensable. Flannel pants should be made long enough for socks to be drawn over them. By enveloping the whole body in flannel the patient is spared the necessity of loading the exterior with thick weighty dresses or heavy overcoats, which fatigue the wearer and confine the act of respiration. Those who are liable to suffer from cold feet, or are susceptible to chilblains, will find thick worsted socks and cloth gaiters a necessity, or thickly lined cloth boots, to come well up the leg. As a prophylactic against chilblains, bathing the feet in salt and water, avoiding tight boots, wearing digitated socks, and changing them whenever the feet are damp from perspiration, &c., keeping the arms warm and the hands dry, will carry many through the winter of a cold climate, who might otherwise suffer much inconvenience and pain from these minor but troublesome ailments.

Ordinary stout skating boots, with broad toes, low heels, and plenty of room inside them, which may be filled up with a cork sock, are suitable both for ladies and gentlemen; they should be well greased every day and always changed immediately after a long walk. Goloshes are useful for short journeys, but cannot be recommended for constant use, on account of confining the perspiration. All clothes should be light in colour, as near grey as the taste will allow. A light colour does not absorb nor radiate heat so much as black; therefore a wearer of grey will be comfortably free from the heat of solar radiation and warmer in the shade. Waistcoats should be lined in the back with flannel, as with modern garments all the protection is in front of the body. (a) If men endeavoured to dispense with the use of braces greater play would be given to the muscles of inspiration. Hats may be of straw for the sunny weather, but light-coloured thin felt answers very well. Furs should not be worn when taking exercise. The ladies' fur tippet can be discarded as superfluous at any time, from the fact of its covering the shoulders only, causing that part of the body to become overheated, and therefore liable to chill. A short list is appended of articles found to be serviceable for these climates:—

One fur or railway rug. One warm ulster, with hood or fur-lined coat for travelling and sleighing. One thin overcoat, a Shetland shawl. Two or three suits of clothes (waistcoats lined). Thick flannel vests and flannel shirts. Flannel night-shirts. Half-a-dozen or more worsted socks. Flannel pants. Cloth or fur gloves with gauntlets. Cork socks. A pair of dark neutral tint spectacles. A few rough bath towels and a flesh glove. One woollen muffler. Two pairs of stout boots (one pair smooth for skating, the other with a few spikes in the soles). A pair of leggings are required for "coasting," unless long boots are taken. One or two pairs of shoes, or thick slippers with heels can be worn indoors with spatts over them. Bootlaces, dubbin, and skates may be added, and for ladies a sunshade and goloshes with cloth tops. A fur foot-warmer or large fur-lined boots are also very useful.

Diet in the Swiss Alps.—The food almost everywhere in Swiss hotels, consists largely of azotised or nitrogenous matter. Many who have visited Switzerland will recollect that much lean meat is eaten, whilst the proportion of animal fats is very small.

(a) With double-breasted apparel a man may have from ten to thirteen thicknesses of woollen clothing in front of him, whilst his back is covered with three layers of wool only.

It is essential to the health and well-being of individuals that a proper proportion of nitrogenous and non-nitrogenous food should be consumed. The latter consists chiefly of starch, fats, sugar, saline substances, and water, which in the ordinary way with meats form the mixed dietary most suitable for man; as the structure of his teeth and past experience indicate. But whilst an almost exact estimate can be formed of the elements necessary for the system to ingest, it must not be forgotten that the quantity and kind of food taken will depend very much on the condition or idiosyncrasy of the consumer. As a general rule, few delicate persons would be capable of effectually digesting the quantity of bread, pastry, milk, and root vegetables, &c., which would be requisite to constitute with the meat eaten, a fair combination of nitrogenous and non-nitrogenous matter, and as there is a marked absence of palatable fat at these places, a little consideration of the means for balancing the needful combination, will conduce to the recovery of health and avert many ill-effects arising from perverted nutrition—as dyspepsia, troubled sleep, a loaded tongue, vitiated secretions, &c.

"Many people," Dr. Pavy remarks, "seem to look upon meat almost as though it formed the only food that really nourished and supplied what is wanted for work. The physician is constantly coming across an expression of this view."

The greatest importance must be attached to the use of fats during winter in the Alps; for it is well-known that the inhabitants of Siberia, Greenland, &c., and all cold countries, eat enormous quantities of these heat-producing materials, without which they would be unable to resist the intense cold of the frigid climate. Sir John Ross observes—" It would be very desirable, indeed, if the men could acquire the taste for Greenland food, since all experience has shown that the large use of oil and fat meats is the true secret of life in these frozen countries."

Dr. Cheadle also lays much stress on the value of fats in cold climates. "One effect of the cold was to give a most ravenous appetite for fat. It is the most valuable part of food in winter, and horses and dogs will not stand work in the cold unless fat." (a)

Besides forming the chief articles of diet which are required for a calorifacient or heat-producing agent, they may almost certainly supply a pabulum for the oxidising process of fever in phthisis to act upon, thereby not only restricting the waste of tissue in that process, but perhaps in some way diverting its occurrence, as is witnessed when cod-liver oil is taken. With an increase in animal food, which can be readily eaten at high cold levels, the appetite being sharpened by exercise and low temperature, the necessity for fats is by no means abated; on the contrary, a physiological demand is created for additional food capable of undergoing the process of oxidation, which cannot be wholly supplied by the lean meat or by starchy and saccharine bodies.

"It appears from the experiments of Pettenkofer and Voit that increasing the proportion of nitrogenous matter in the food determines an increased absorption of oxygen by the lungs. Nitrogenous matter it is which starts the changes occurring in the system, and the suggestion presents itself that upon the amount of nitrogenous matter may, to some extent, depend the application of oxygen to the oxidation of fatty matter. Under this view the success of Mr. Banting's system may be due, not exclusively to the restriction of the principles that tend to produce fat, but in part, also, to an increased oxidising action promoted by the large amount of nitrogenous matter consumed." (Pavy).

Let us draw attention to the substances at these health resorts that furnish the calorifacient group of alimentary

---

(a) "The North West Passage by Land." Viscount Milton and Dr. Cheadle.

principles. Disregarding the fat produced by a complicated metamorphosis of the carbo-hydrates and a small part of the nitrogenous food ingested (a) the main articles of diet from which fat is derived, would be butter and milk. About 1 oz. of the former at breakfast, and 2 pints of milk during the twenty-four hours together furnish at the most 2·6 ozs. of fat, allowing from ½ oz. to 1 oz. for that contained in the lean meat with gravies, &c., 3 to 3½ ozs., are obtained. It is doubtful if this is sufficient with exercise and low temperature, nor is it to be recommended that those with poor appetites should drink more milk. Persons should eat plentifully of butter at breakfast, especially as that meal is not a substantial one.

It would also be very advantageous to continue taking cod-liver oil if it had been found to agree in England, for reasons that are plainly apparent. Should the stomach have been unable to digest it hitherto, trial should again be made in a cold climate, as it might be then more easily assimilated, its oxidation being assisted by the increased proportion of nitrogenous material ingested. A good time for taking it is immediately after lunch or dinner in a glass of marsala, or in milk half an hour after a meal, commencing with one teaspoonful, and gradually increasing the dose.

Pancreatine and pancreatine emulsion are sometimes valuable in assisting the digestion, and malt extracts also. All these substances can be looked upon as supplementary to diet, and not as medicines. If cod-liver oil is objectionable, butter should be eaten at every meal, or cream be made use of.

To further demonstrate the virtue in cod-liver oil, fat, and

(a) It is questionable, if with the low temperature in the Alps, phthisical persons should be physiologically compelled to maintain much of the body-heat by the carbo-hydrates, as the changes in their principles previous to their becoming calorifacient take place in the liver ; and the function of that organ is often impaired in phthisis.

butter, the following table taken from Frankland, will give a clear idea of their force-producing value.

Name of Food.	Per cent. of Water present.	Force-producing value.		
		In units of heat.	In kilogrammetres of Force.	
			When burnt in oxygen.	When oxidised in the body.
Cod-liver oil...	—	9107	3857	3857
Beef-fat	—	9069	3841	3841
Butter	—	7264	3077	3077
Cocoa-nibs	—	6873	2911	2902
Cheese (Cheshire)	24	4647	1969	1846
Isinglass	—	4520	1914	1550
Bread-crust	—	4459	1888	—
Oatmeal	—	4004	1696	1665
Flour	—	3936	1669	1627
Pea-meal	—	3936	1667	1598
Arrowroot	—	3912	1657	1657
Ground rice..	—	3813	1615	1591
Yolk of egg...	47·0	3423	1449	1400
Lump sugar...	—	3348	1418	1418
Grape sugar (commercial)	—	3277	1388	1388
Hard-boiled egg	62·3	2383	1009	966
Bread-crumb...	44·0	2231	945	910
Ham, lean (boiled)	54·4	1980	839	711
Mackerel	70·5	1789	758	683
Beef (lean)	70·5	1567	664	604
Veal (lean)	70·9	1314	556	496
Guinness's stout	88·4	1076	455	455
Potatoes	73·0	1013	429	422
Whiting	80·0	904	383	335
Bass's ale (alcohol reckoned)	88·4	775	328	328
White of egg	86·3	671	284	244
Milk	87·0	662	280	266
Apples	82·0	660	280	273
Carrots	86·0	527	223	220
Cabbage	88·5	434	184	178

In the event of high temperature supervening, the digestion of meats is greatly interfered with, and the usual diet stands in need of modification, as the nitrogenous matter will, if excessive, embarrass the digestive powers, and prove an encumbrance to the stomach, leading to further complications, which may be avoided by substituting food of a different nature that has not to undergo such a complicated process of absorption and elimination. For this purpose, milk and raw eggs are to be chiefly relied on, with beef-tea, soups, jellies, light puddings, toast, biscuits, and farinaceous substances, as arrowroot, or one of the numerous "foods." By this regimen, bearing in mind that the system requires much less nourishment when the body is at rest, an ample dietary is furnished. During bad weather, also, when but little exercise can be undertaken, and confinement indoors is called for, diminished diet proves of some service, not only to the comfort of the patient, but to his general condition, and, consequently, the local state of disease.

On the cold, dry days, with outdoor exercise, the appetite can be wholly satisfied, with safety and advantage, for it is on these occasions that the "push" is given to nutrition, and any excess in nourishment is more likely to be burnt up or assimilated in the system, to maintain heat, produce force, or counterbalance waste or change.

As the breakfast is not a substantial meal, it will be perceived that the latter part of the day, between noon and 8 p.m., is the period principally occupied by the digestive process, the remaining sixteen hours, therefore, will, in the case of delicate persons, prove to be a great tax on the force and heat-producing powers unless sustained in some way or other. Although it is impossible to lay down rules to apply to every one, a short dietary table for an ordinary case of loss of flesh can be modified to suit the temperament or capacity of any individual, bearing in mind that in many instances "suitable diet" is a matter of experiment.

Regimen at the Swiss Health Resorts.

7 or 7.30 a.m.—Warm milk, ½ litre.

8 or 8.30 a.m.—Breakfast: Tea, coffee, or chocolate, ½ litre; bread, butter, honey. Extras not provided *en pension*—eggs, cold meat, bacon, omelette, &c.

Noon or 1 p.m.—Lunch: Soup, meats, fresh vegetables, sweets, cheese, a glass of red wine, or wine and water (½ pint).

4 or 4.30 p.m.—Warm milk, ½ pint, with a biscuit, or other light refreshment, as tea, coffee, with bread and butter.

5.30 or 6 p.m.—Dinner: Soup, fish, or *entrées*, meats, vegetables, sweets, cheese, red wine or wine and water (½ litre).

9 p.m.—Supper not provided *en pension*. Milk, ½ pint, with biscuit, &c., or beef-tea, or some "food" prepared with milk.

A glass of milk, with a biscuit, may also be taken sometimes at 11 a.m. if it is found to agree.

If night-sweats occur, nourishment should be taken at frequent intervals, especially during the night. Stimulants are efficacious at these times—whisky, rum, or cognac; but spirits should always be mixed with milk or egg, or both combined. Their efficiency seems to be increased in this way. Neat spirits as a "*petit verre*" cannot be recommended with much benefit unless there is food in the stomach. Brand's extract of meat and Liebig's, are suitable also. These can be mixed together, when they form a better and more natural beef-tea, than when taken separately. The Veltliner wine drunk with meals will act as a good astringent. A frequent cause of perspiration at night is an excessive quantity of clothes on the bed. The usual eiderdown quilt should not cover the patient if night-sweats are frequent. A flannel night-shirt is of great service on these occasions, and the

temperature of the bedroom ought never to rise over fifty-five
degrees. Fifty to fifty-five degrees is generally found to be a
comfortable temperature in winter.

Exercise, Meals, Sleep, etc.—It is unnecessary to point
out the need for individual management in this matter.
Much will depend on the state of health and capability for
exertion. One rule can, however, be laid down—viz., keep
in the open air as much as possible. This will of itself
entail a fair amount of movement, but if the state of the
lungs does not preclude skating, coasting, tobogganing, (a) or
walking ascents—care must, of course, be taken in beginning
exercise gradually. A state of breathlessness or fatigue must
never be permitted, nor must the body be allowed to cool
rapidly if perspiring.

The time available at these altitudes in the depth of
winter is somewhat limited for delicate persons, as the sun at
this time of the year remains but a short time in the valleys
(five or six hours). It is therefore incumbent on those
seeking health to make the most of this time, and when
in-doors to breathe as much fresh air as can be admitted with
comfort. Bedroom windows can be left a little open if the
nights are clear, and the heat of the stoves regulated accord-
ingly. In giving an outline of personal hygienic management a description of how the day may be passed will be of
some assistance.

At 6.30 or 7 a.m. the stove should be lighted, and a
half-litre of milk, warm from the cow, be brought to the
bedside of the patient. After drinking this, an hour's sleep
may be had. If a cold bath be prohibited, a rapid sponging

(a) The term "toboggan" for the Canadian sled has grown into use
in Switzerland, but is entirely a misnomer. The toboggan may be
described as a flat plank turned up at one end, and is used for travelling
over snow slopes, but the "sled" is in all respects a minature sleigh and
runs on frozen roads or hardened snow.

of the chest and back, followed by friction, is of great
service in keeping the skin in a healthy condition. A fairly
vigorous patient may have a cold bath, or the chill may be
taken off; but precaution must be observed in having the
air of the bedroom at this time fresh and warm (not below
55 degs. F.), so that the deep inspirations caused by the
shock of cold to the skin shall not take in the used-up
bedroom air. A bath or sponging may be tolerated in many
cases, provided it takes place *immediately on rising*, while
the body is hot. If the skin be allowed to cool down by
tardiness in preparing for the bath the water will feel intensely cold. Slight dumb-bell movements may be executed
when dressed, throwing the shoulders back and taking deep
inspirations. Soon after breakfast, which is taken 8.30 or
9 a.m., the patient should get out for a walk, making a slight
ascent if not too short of breath; and returning at 11 a.m.
for a glass of warm milk. The afternoons are mostly spent
in sitting out of doors, skating, coasting, walking or sleighing,
the latter is not to be recommended in very cold weather.
Another half-pint of milk can be drunk in the afternoon, or
a little light refreshment such as tea or coffee will do no
harm, the patient being generally able to determine if it can
be taken with benefit. If he finds it too much fluid, a less
quantity of thin cream might be substituted. Dr. Symes
Thompson gives a short piece of advice free from mysticism
on the subject of exercise in the Alps (a):—" Those in health
need few restraints, but for those with active lung disease
sudden exertion on arrival should be discouraged lest it lead
to hæmorrhage. If there is active disease or hæmorrhagic
tendency or moist sounds in the lung, the patient should sit
out in the sun till dry sounds replace moist ones. He may
then walk on the level, or skate, or gently stroll up and down

(a) "On the Winter Health Resorts of the Alps." E. Symes
Thompson, M.D.

hill, thus causing deep inspiration. Quiet skating can be indulged in by almost all. Tobogganing is more severe, as patients are apt to talk and laugh when walking up hill. This is very good for the vigorous, as it expands the chest. Lawn tennis is suited only for the strongest, in whom lung disease is quiescent."

The dinner hour varies in different hotels from 5·30 to 7 o'clock; 6 or 6·30 p.m. is a very good hour. Food should be taken leisurely, and masticated well. Half an hour's rest before and after meals facilitates digestion. The evenings are spent in various ways. Davos possesses a theatre and concert room (*a*) and amateur theatricals are got up at the hotels with concerts, tableaux vivants, &c. It would be a great boon if, on the occasions of such gatherings, artificial means were provided for the purification of contaminated air similar to those used in the recreation-rooms of the Maloja. With the intense external cold, air cannot be plentifully admitted to dilute the effete products of respiration, &c., therefore, although entertainments in crowded rooms generally conduce to a healthy frame of mind, and tend to banish despondency, evils originate if sanitary precautions are neglected.

With respect to the length of time for sleep, the temperament and habits of the individual will have to be considered. The old dictum of six hours for a man, and seven for a woman will scarcely commend itself to most people, nor does experience teach us that any definite duration of time for mental and physical rest can be determined with exactitude. The intensity of muscular, mental, or nervous exhaustion during the day will in all cases influence the desire for repose. Cold also predisposes to sleep, as may be witnessed in hybernating animals. Some human beings also hybernate. It will not be too much to say that eight or nine hours slumber in winter, at

(*a*) This handsome *Salon* at the Kurhaus is ventilated by a calorifère.

these cold staticus, is near the mark; remembering that nothing is to be gained by remaining in bed in a semi-state of wakefulness after this time is past.

If smoking cannot be entirely given up, the quantity of tobacco used should be cut down as low as possible. Cigarette smoking should certainly be discontinued by those whose lungs are affected, as the habit generally acquired of inhaling the smoke or passing it through the nasal passages, proves very irritating to the mucous membrane, and is more injurious to the throat and lungs than the same portion of tobacco smoked in a pipe.

CHAPTER VI.

The South West End of the Upper Engadine.

The MALOJA.—Since the development of Davos Platz into an Alpine Winter resort and a rapid growth in size and population, other places have sprung up having strong claims to be considered equal, if not superior, to that well-known but rather well-filled little town. St. Moritz revives an ancient effort to attract people in winter, this time with some success, the Kulm Hôtel having more than a hundred and fifty guests living there during the past season. Wiesen the picturesque, with its ponderous flanks and countless pine trees, is on a fair way to offer health to a limited number who desire quietude and the charms of country life. The milder temperature and extreme calmness give a special character to this resort, which renders it suitable as a change at the end of the winter season for those who have been living at a higher level.

It is indispensable for the reputation of the high valleys in Switzerland that more places spring up for the " winter cure," as it is notorious to those who give real attention to the subject that, although these places increase in size, population, and independence, individual and collective energy is needed to keep pace with overcrowding and to preserve the

L'HÔTEL-KURSAAL DE LA MALOJA.

clean air of the Alpine heights free from contamination. As but few hours can be spent out of the house in winter, it is imperative that hotels which harbour a number of delicate individuals in search of health within their walls should be rendered perfect in a sanitary point of view, both as regards drainage and ventilation. Of how much therapeutic value must that air be, which in five or six hours can not only neutralise the ill-effects of a contaminated atmosphere for the remainder of the day and night, but can, in numerous instances, favour an almost miraculous recovery. Heretofore, the curative properties of these climates have only been developed to a fraction of their full power; and whilst the restorative agent has lien at the closed doors and double windows of over-loaded hotels, patients have been sent home cured in spite of what would seem to be to on-lookers either an under estimation of the true antidote or the popular disinclination to incur any expense for efficient sanitary arrangements.

These drawbacks, however, have now been met by the construction on the Maloja plateau of a large Kursaal (designed especially for winter residence by M. Jules Rau, a Belgian architect), fitted with arrangements for the propulsion and extraction of air throughout the building, as well as for the addition of ozone to the atmosphere of the corridors and some of the large salons. The latter is effected by the surplus electricity at command in use for the electric lighting of the building. The Kursaal, which may be considered unique in all sanitary arrangements, faces the lake of Sils, between which and the N.E. façade lies the *parc*, and the S.W. side of the building a large garden (in all, 13 acres), with skating-rink, pavilions, &c. A theatre-salon is semi-detached from the main corridor to guard against any transmission of sound to the interior of the house. This structure is also warmed and ventilated by propulsion and extrac-

F

tion, but in a slightly modified manner to that of the general plan.

An entirely new departure has been taken as regards the drainage of these mountain resorts, a plan has been adopted by which it is impossible for any sewer-gas to enter the dwelling. The main difficulty in these climates—viz., the freezing of the water supply to *cabinets*, has been overcome, and each *cabinet*, *urinoir*, &c., is efficiently trapped, ventilated with the external air, and warmed in winter.

It is anticipated, and with some reason, that what has been termed the air-cure will be exhibited in its true meaning, and that results hitherto unattainable where "air-nourishment" is the essentiality will be achieved with greater rapidity and success than in many other health-resorts where but little mindfulness is bestowed on a point of such signal importance.

As much attention is devoted at the present time to all matters connected with hygiene, notably that section relating to ventilation, a description of the system in use at the Kursaal Hotel will be given further on.

MALOJA.—The meaning of this word has caused much speculation, and as various constructions have been put on the origin of "mal" and "loggia," the opinions of two Swiss authorities on such subjects will be interesting. Dr. Killias, of Coire, who was kind enough to furnish the author with information on the subject, writes as follows:—"The meaning of the word Maloja or Maloggia (locally Malöja or Malöggia, pronounced Malögia) is as difficult of explanation as innumerable other local names. The Rhaetic names are mostly of very old origin, being derived, it is said, from the Etrusk, Keltic, and other antique Rhaetic origins. As regards receiving the apparently Italian or Latin origin, one must be very cautious, much nonsense having been already published thoughtlessly, e.g., the explanation of Celerina as "celer" oenus. Now there the river Inn does not run any faster than in the neighbourhood. This name has simply been changed in favour of the well-sounding Italian word, the real and true name being Romansch, "Schlarina," as found on all old maps, but falsely explained latterly by a Latin etymology. The first mention of the name Maloja I find in a list of references of the Bishopric at Coire (edited between 1290 and 1298 where it is written Malöggia). Campell, in 1572, writes Malögia, and explains the name after the manner of the scholars of that time, 'Majores Juliæ, videlicet alpes.' Now the name of Julier has nothing to do with Julius Cæsar, who never came to Rhaetia. Sererhand (1742) speaks of Maloja, and mentions an inn which stood there. No doubt at those times no first-rate lodgings could be had, but in all probability no worse than at the villages round about; therefore the explanation of 'bad-lodging' is an idle word-play. The root 'mal' has clearly two meanings—I. Latin, in which case it is often found at the end: Via mala, Pass mal, Val mala; not Malvia, Malpass, Malval. II. There must be quite another word at the bottom, probably Celtic, as there are a great number of names with the 'mal' at the beginning, and where the meaning of 'bad' has no sense at all—Malenco, Maladers, Malans, Mals, Malenz (Vintschgau), Malaer; then others not in the Canton of the Grisons, Malbun, to be explained, 'bad good'! Malfrag, Malgera, &c., &c. I cannot say absolutely that the 'mal' is derived from the Celtic 'mael,' a mountain, is right or not, but I decidedly refuse the Latin signification in these cases.

"Some time since a Mr. Pallioppi, of Celerina, compiled a Romansch vocabulary, which ought to have been printed; unfortunately the author died before this could take place, his son, however, occupies himself with the subject, and would be able to give you more exact details."

The Rev. Emil Pallioppi writes:—

"My late father takes the name Maloja from the Celtic. Malógia, Malöggia, Maloja, either taken from the Cymric 'moelang' or 'moelôg,' which means a place rich of Cills, as is the case in that part of the Engadine, or synonymous with 'mullach,' top of a mountain or culm; wherefrom also comes the word 'mualach' (mólac) with the signification of road, pass. The transitions from *u* or *o* to *a*, and *vice versâ*, have no difficulty at all, because those three vowels in Celtic are often used one for another (*vide* Pallioppi). Or the word is composed from 'mala' a hill, mountain, top of a mountain, culm, and 'oiche,' water. In fact is, the small hill or pass on the Lake of Sils, or not far away."

The **MALOJA PLATEAU** is situated at the higher extremity of the Upper Engadine, and is well protected from northerly, easterly, and southerly winds. Facing the plateau is the lake of Sils; the largest in the chain of lakes between Maloja and St. Moritz. In contrast with the glassiness of its tranquil waters, and the clear blue of the sky, are the rugged crags of the higher Alps, clothed below with red firs and larches. The site is considered by many to be the most romantic and picturesque part of the Engadine.

On the eastern wing of the lake and plateau lie the Bernina chain: comprising the loftiest mountains of the Grisons and the whole of Switzerland, matted with glaciers and snow fields to an extent of more than 350 square miles. The slopes of the Corvatsch, Surlej, and Della Margna (their peaks elevated to ten and eleven thousand feet), abut on the lake of Sils, and eastern side of the plateau, protecting the lower ground. Opposite and rounding towards the northeast the rough broadside of Lunghino, Gravasalvas, and Materdell are in close proximity. To the south the Muretto, Dei Rosso, Del Forno, and Salecina rear their summits to heights of 10,000 feet, whilst a mile or so to the south-west is seen the prominent Piz Lizzone and the serrated crests on the eastern ridge of the Val Bregaglia.

By these shelters the plateau is screened from harsh upper currents of air. The thalwind or valley-wind, which blows in every Swiss valley, seldom exceeds a force of one degree Beaufort scale, is by no means insupportable, and dies away in force and frequence when snow covers the adjacent regions. At this season, and when the lake of Sils freezes, greater calm prevails, and the locality partakes of that Alpine stillness and sunshine which allows the most delicate individuals to be exposed to a low temperature without feeling the sensation of cold.

Preceding and during a fall of snow in the mountains of Switzerland, storms are not uncommon, alternating with lulls and blasts of wind. Commonly these proceed from a southerly or south-westerly direction and bring with them the peculiar changes in the atmosphere, which have given rise to a special name for southerly currents of air, viz., föhn wind. This föhn, which is considered the pernicious wind for invalids is rarely perceived at the S.W. end of the Engadine, its peculiar characteristics being tempered by the high altitude, and by passage over a portion of the Bernina snow fields and glaciers. In this way the temperature of a southerly current is greatly reduced, and the commencement of the föhn shorn of its sultriness. The rapid rise in temperature at the onset of a southerly wind were not at all common during the past two winters, nor was there ever noticed within the Kursaal an atmosphere too dry for healthy respiration in doors.

One of the most important features of Alpine climate—and one which unquestionably acts as an adjuvant in the chemical process of the natural and healthy change taking place in the blood discs—is the amount and duration of sunlight. Were it not for the transparent air and powerful sun the high Alps would be quite unsuited to delicate people. By reason of the direct chemical action of light, and the increased time afforded for out-door amusement and exercise which a longer day admits of, an additional hour's sunlight during the short days of December and January is an inconceivable advantage, both for the mind as well as the body. The inequality, in this respect, of Davos, Wiesen, and St. Moritz, with the Maloja, is due, as may be supposed, to the configuration of the surrounding mountains. If a slice could be taken off the Jacobshorn at Davos, and the Stulsergrat, at Wiesen, the sun would flood those districts before half-past ten, on the shortest day.

St. Moritz at this time loses the sun at 3 p.m., and although it rises during the middle of February at a quarter to eight, it sets at 3.50 p.m. The sunset of the Maloja on this date takes place at 4.30 p.m., and during the months of December and January the Hotel-Kursaal has more than one hour's sunshine longer than Davos, Wiesen, or St. Moritz. In respect of duration of sunlight, Pontresina still exceeds the Maloja, but does not enjoy the *late sunset of the latter*. At the end the reader will find the sun-hours given for the various health resorts during the winter months. Sunrise and sunset take place on the first day of January as follows :

		Sunrise.	Sunset.
	Maloja	9.35	3.45 P.M.
	Wiesen	10.35	3.45 ,,
(a)	Pontresina	8.30	3.10 ,,
(a)	St. Moritz	10.0	3.5 ,,
	Davos Platz	10.3	3.0 ,,
(b)	Andermatt	11.45	3.15 ,,

(a) Taken from the houses on the main road of the village (Dr. Ludwig's "Ober-Engadin").
(b) Reported by Dr. Schmid.

It will be seen that Wiesen and Pontresina stand next to the Maloja, the late departure of the sun being of most consequence.

The necessity for exposure to Alpine solar rays in the treatment of various complaints, is well illustrated by cases of anæmia among some of the domestics employed in hotels at these levels. Attracted by the rumours of cure in anæmia they seek employment at some health station, but being principally confined to kitchens and shady places their anæmia rests with but little improvement. The case with nurse-girls is different as they very soon gain a healthy tint, being constantly in the open air.

Another advantageous feature of this part of the Engadine, is the vast extent of level ground which admits of exercise being taken without fatigue. After the breathing becomes freer and there is a tendency for the chest to expand, tobogganing and gentle ascents can be undertaken. For the more vigorous a descent into the Bergell Valley on a sled is one of the finest runs in Switzerland. Skating of course, can be indulged in by those who are equal to the pastime; a good rink is in course of preparation, whilst the lake of Sils is but 300 yards from the Hotel. It is in the choice of amusements and graduation of exercise where judgment ought to be shown. During summer-time more variety in out-door sports and games can be pursued, mountaineering, boating, fishing, lawn-tennis, &c., and consequently more care must be taken in refraining from over-exertion. The long evenings of winter can be enlivened by healthy indoor amusements, as fresh air and ozone are supplied to the theatre-salon as well as to other recreation rooms, and a clean atmosphere is breathed day and night.

The climate can be described in the general terms of all Swiss high level stations, viz., a stimulating, bracing, tonic, and cold climate; increasing the power of the heart and other muscles, expanding the chest and exciting the nervous and

glandular systems into healthy activity. The Maloja shows a
more equable temperature than Davos, and the winter season
lasts a little longer, which is a great advantage to those who
make a change to lower levels, as the weather would probably
be more settled the further spring is advanced. The rapid
rises in temperature caused by the föhn in mid-winter are by
no means so frequent or so high as in the narrower situations.
It is not pretended that any part of the Upper Engadine is,
on the whole, as calm as the Davos valley : the latter is so by
reason of its being narrower (limiting the sunshine, and
favouring stagnation of air); but what one health resort loses
on one hand it gains on the other.

Omitting the occasional storms that sweep over the whole
of the Alps, the gentle and bracing currents of air which move
everywhere in the Upper Engadine, although not suited to
serious forms of illness, are pleasant by reason of their dryness,
and prove of the greatest benefit to those who have sufficient
strength to walk. In all the narrow valleys it must
not be forgotten that the dead-calm days and burning
sun are usually precursors of the föhn wind, which
has peculiarities of so much importance to delicate
persons.

During mid-winter a dip of over 3,200 feet can be
made in an hour and a-half to Promotogno, where there is a
good hotel ; and the Italian climate of Chiavenna (1,090 feet)
can be reached in less than three hours, if the upper level
appears to disagree. This facility in being able to quit the
highlands without a prolonged, and in cases of illness, a
dangerous journey from any other Alpine station, cannot be
over-rated. Doubtless there are instances in which any
climate, either cold or temperate, does not always effect the
salubrious change anticipated ; it then becomes a question of
the utmost importance to an invalid, how to escape without
incurring risk. In the present instance the dangers of
moving, even in the depth of winter, are at a minimum. A

drive to the lake of Como requires less time than it takes to reach Davos from Landquart.

The soil and vegetation of the Maloja are of the usual character found at these altitudes, a thin, rich, dark incrustation of the former, rapidly absorbing moisture. The bed of the plateau (formed by an ancient recession of the lake of Sils) consists of peaty mould, resting on a layer of gravel. Up to a height of 1,000 feet and 2,000 feet above the level ground the slopes on the eastern side are covered with larches and red pines. The western side is rugged, large boulders and crags being interspersed with patches of nutritious short grass. On the plateau itself, and the little hills adjoining, are dwarf *melèzes* (red pines), heath, and cranberry bushes.

The coldest part of the Engadine is near Bevers; the temperature in winter becomes a little higher as we approach the Maloja, owing to the fact that its south-west end terminates in an abrupt fall of 1,200 feet (*a*) into the extensive valley of Bergell, which after passing Promontogno terminates near Chiavenna in Italy, eighteen miles distant; the Italian frontier being twelve miles from the Maloja. To the proximity of a channel at this end for milder air to mount and replace the denser and colder strata, the deviation in temperature may be attributed.

The difference, however, with the several Alpine health resorts lies, not so much in their grades of temperature, as in their sanitary characters, especially as regards the purity of internal air. As the term "air-cure" (luft kurort) has rightly or wrongly grown into use, it will be expedient to include in this chapter a description of the special appliances which have been placed in this modern building with a view of furnishing a larger breathing space to its inmates.

The system admits of being adjusted to suit any temperature or degree of humidity of external atmosphere. The

(*a*) The precipitous descent is cut by a road with sixteen zig-zags.

calculation by M. Cortella of the volume of air provided for each individual, shows the possibility of supplying 100 mètres cubes (3,500 cubic feet) per hour for each person, supposing the Kursaal to contain 500 individuals. By the double means of propulsion and extraction furnished to each chamber this breathing space exceeds by 0·6 times the estimate given by one of the greatest authorities for ventilating soldiers' barracks at night, (a) and the same care has been exhibited in ventilating the basement of the house as in ventilating the bed and sitting rooms.

In the basement beneath the theatre and concert room, situated apart from the main building, are placed three *chaudières* in which steam is generated to a low pressure (one to three atmospheres). This steam is conveyed to forty-nine *batteries*, distributed throughout the basement, where it traverses a series of pipes and flanges attached to increase the surface of heat. A *batterie* is made up of twenty pipes enclosed in a case, through which air is drawn from the outside of the building, previously passing through wire gauze. This air receives heat by passing over the steam pipes, whilst the steam is condensed, and returns as tepid water to the *chaudière* for the economy of fuel. Within these *batteries* are contrivances for moistening the dry external air to a healthful degree of humidity in harmony with the increase of temperature and hygrometric condition of the atmosphere; and by a simple contrivance the air of one or more rooms can be medicated with volatilised remedial agents, as leading from each *batterie* are tubes supplying the rooms with air, the quantity being controlled by valves below and a sliding valve in each chamber.

(a) In barracks, 30 mètres cubes, per hour during the day; 60 by night. Workshops, 60 mètres cubes. Schools, 30. Hospitals, 80. (Morin).

CHAUFFAGE ET VENTILATION

Cortella, Co:

▨ Batteries de Chauffe.

☐ Entrée de l'air extérieur.

☐ Sortie de l'air vicié.

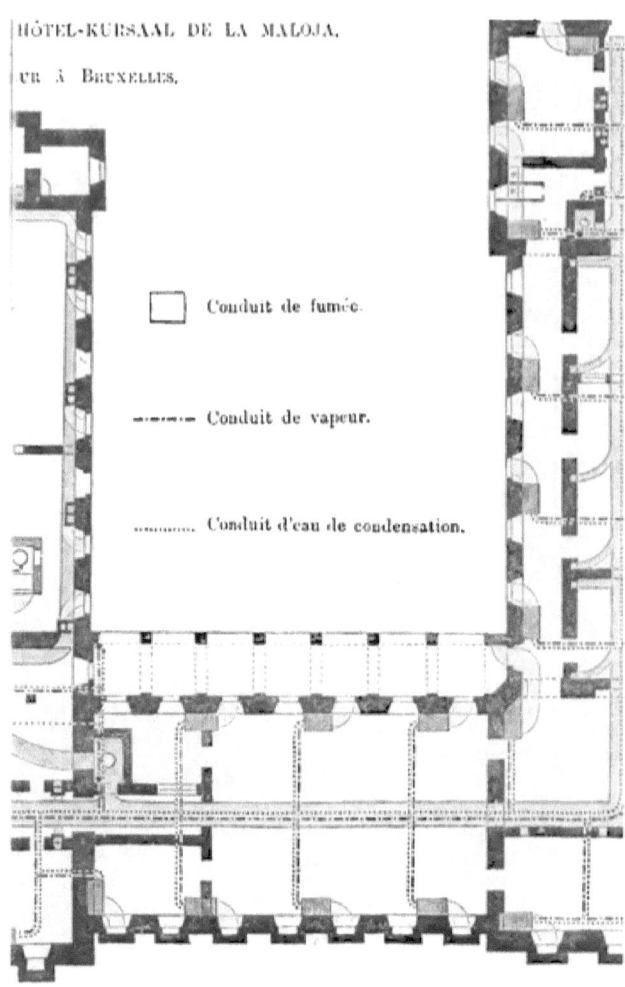

US-SOL.

The ascending power of the warmed air at a temperature of 50° centigrade (122° Fahr.) raises it through the conduits to each room in the house, where it enters a dormitory at the topmost storey, having an agreeable temperature, and at a sufficient rate to change the air of a bedroom once every two or three hours. In the theatre, smoking and billiard rooms, and public salons, a necessary number of conduits are provided for renewing the atmosphere at least once every two hours.

Each delivery tube is fitted with a sliding valve which can be adjusted at pleasure according to a degree of heat desirable for comfort.

To allow of the escape of used-up air two tubes of exit are placed in a chamber, one under the bed for the winter ventilation, another near the ceiling, used in summer to exhaust from the warmer stratum of air. These exit tubes are in connection with an iron casing surrounding the main flue of the *chaudières*, that acts as an extraction shaft for the foul air of the central portion of the building. The kitchen chimney acts in this manner for another part of the house and together with the flue of the confectionery and that of the bakehouse, placed in the basement, aspirate the air of other rooms into the double chimneys. As the upward motion in these extraction shafts would scarcely be forcible and rapid enough during summer time to effectually withdraw the air from so many chambers, and as perchance some air might find its way back again to the upper stories, a contrivance with steam tubes is fixed in the space beneath the roof to again heat and thereby promote the ascent of foul air and so accelerate its escape externally.

Every corridor, salon, bed-room, and *cabinet* in the house is thus ventilated, and the atmosphere of any special chamber can be medicated at will by placing an antiseptic agent in the air-tube supplying the apartment: being volatilised at a temperature of 50° centigrade, the product is rapidly carried to its destination without tainting the air of other rooms by its odour, as the escape will take place in the exit shafts, each chamber having its own separate ventilation by three channels—one inlet and two outlet (one for the escape of warm impure air, the other for the cooler air near the floor) By the simple adjustment of the valves in a room, the temperature can be regulated with nicety. Even in summer, if the *batteries* are not heated, extraction will go on as usual; and the windows may be opened without interfering in any way with the general ventilation of the house.

It will easily be seen that with this system various therapeutic agents of undoubted importance are placed under immediate control, viz. :—

        1. Temperature.
        2. Moistened fresh air.
        3. Volatilised remedial agents.

In addition, ozone generated by a powerful apparatus placed in the vestibule, permeates the corridors, &c., and passes to the théâtre-salon by means of a "blower" and tubes.

The ozoniser draws off its electricity from the main current of the incandescent lights. After passing through an inductorium, a current of enormous tension (300,000 volts) is produced and distributed over the surface of numerous glass plates coated with tin-foil. Air is forced between the glass plates and through the ozoniser by means of a "blower" driven by a water-motor.

In no sense does there appear to be a contra-indication of the summer Alpine climate for persons with chest complaints, that is with some of the early phases of phthisis, not those with hopeless advanced symptoms, and who are in a feeble irritable condition, with high fever, and incapacity for gentle exercises. The determination of suitable cases for the high altitudes, both in summer and winter can be roughly gauged by the amount of physical power conserved, taken in con-

COUPE TRANSVERSALE SUR L'ARRIERE DE GAUCHE.

☐   Entrée de l'air extérieur.

☐   Air chauffé.

☐   Air vicié.

────   Conduit de vapeur.

··········   Eau Condencée.

H   Ventilation d'hiver.

E   Ventilation d'été.

COUPE ET DÉTAILS D'UNE BATTERIE.

COUPE SUIVANT I. J.

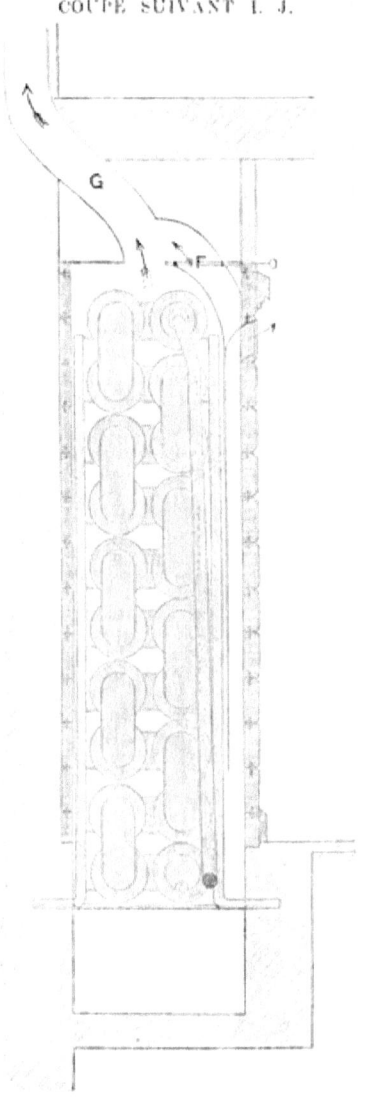

- Maçonnerie.
- Enveloppes des batteries.
- Appareils de chauffage.
- Attaches et supports.
- Vase de saturation.
- Prise d'air.
- Conduit de vapeur.

A Purgeur.

B Robinet.

C Tuyau d'écoulement de l'eau.

D Trappe montée à charnières.

E Registres pour modérer.

F Valve de mélange.

G Conduits d'air.

H Idem aux étages.

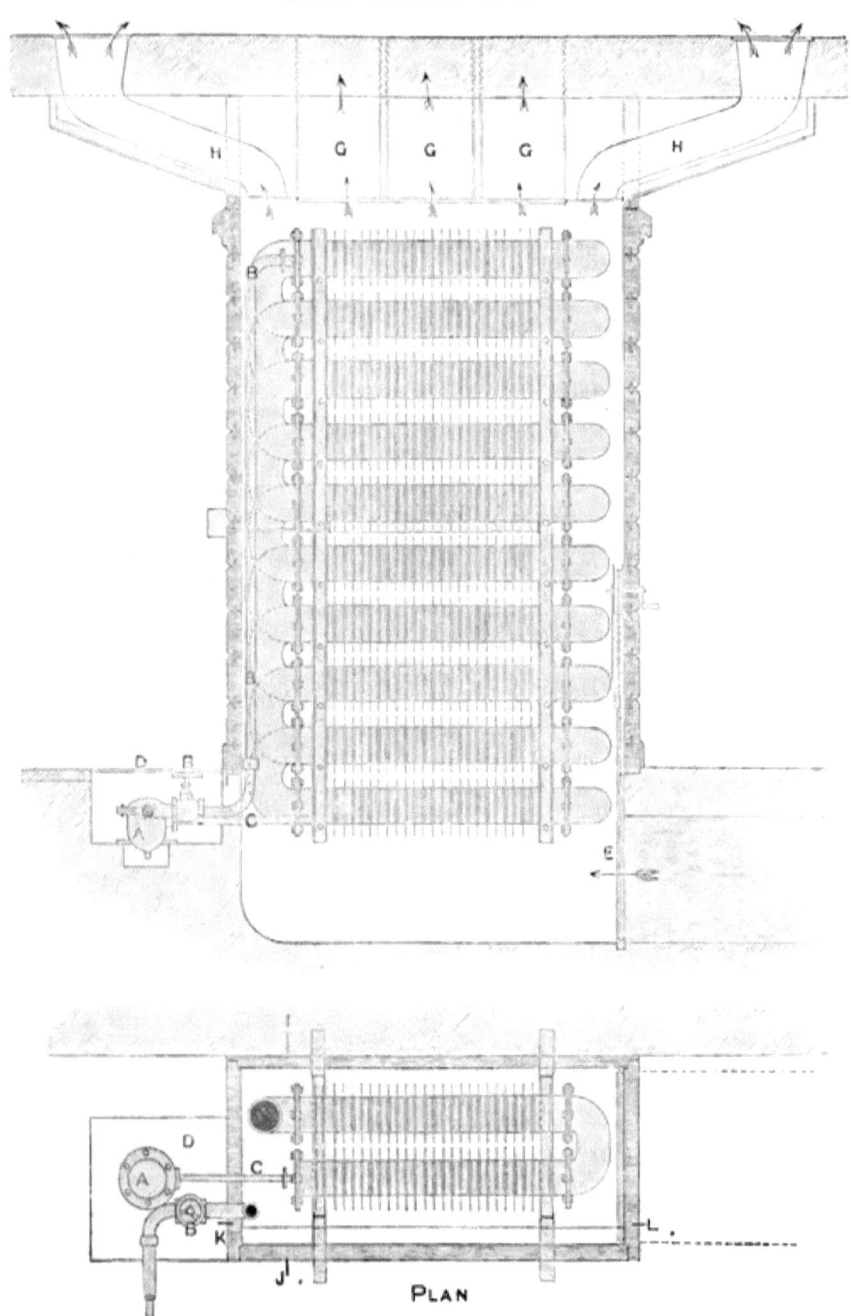

junction with the duration and apparent rate with which consolidation or softening is advancing. The slow scrofulous forms and fibroid conditions receive undoubted benefit, but these must not be complicated with secondary lesions.

A little misapprehension exists on the duration of what is known as the " summer season." Fashion has led the custom of visiting the Engadine in the months of July and August: the majority of persons entertaining an impression that those are the only months to see the Engadine in all its beauty, and at the same time acquire the succour of its restorative climate. This is quite a false notion formed on no foundation of reality. The months of June and September are sometimes among the best that can be spent in the Alps at these altitudes, and the air at the same time carries with it the remarkable invigorating agencies which characterise the mountain climate. The worst period of the year is the snow-melting, occurring some time during the month of April; but this can scarcely be termed a dangerous season, even to the most delicate persons, provided that ordinary precautions are taken in keeping the feet dry and not incurring thoughtless exposure to inclement weather. This applies equally to the introductory snow-falls and storms preceding the settled weather of winter. Invalids must guard against unnecessary exposure everywhere, both on the Riviera and in the Alps, although it would perhaps be less injurious to face a mild Alpine snow-storm than remain shut up in a badly ventilated room in a southern health resort.

The length of time, also, needed for a permanent recovery of lost strength or health, has ever been considered too short to carry with it a firm re-establishment of exhausted energy. A summer month spent in the Engadine—with assiduous regard to diet, exercise, sleep, and medical treatment—should, in almost every instance, be prolonged to six weeks *at least*; longer if time permitted. The lengthened stay would in the long run, be an economy of time as far as health was con-

cerned, and prove a greater satisfaction to doctors and patients
alike. Force of a more lasting and durable nature would be
accumulated, the system settle down in a more staple condition, with enlarged powers of resistance to morbid impressions than if the treatment be suddenly relinquished to return
to old occupations and former habits.

It is true that physiological changes take place with great
rapidity and completeness. A good indication of such being
the case is the demand made by nature for more fuel, shown
by the increased appetite, by the skin acting under the
stimulus of baths, the kidneys and the whole glandular
system being awakened into activity, blood changes quickened
and amplified, and above all, the perception that the
capacity for mental and physical exertion is extended, but
if a departure is made immediately improvement of the
health is attained and strength begins to be felt, some
disappointment may eventually be experienced, and the
climate be discredited by the transient effects of too short a
stay to allow the frame to be seasoned in the new conditions,
or undergo the peculiar alteration known as acclimatisation.
This is especially noticeable in anæmia and chlorosis, where
the blood changes take place rather rapidly, and a hue of
health is acquired in a few weeks leading to an erroneous
conclusion that a permanent cure is effected, whereas a
further time is needed for its completeness. In chronic
cases, either of catarrhs (pulmonary, gastric, or uterine),
phthisis, anæmia, some abdominal affections, and even dyspepsia, a medical mind is aware of the value of prudent
management after the disappearance of symptoms. Whilst
it is evident that in constitutional affections, such as scrofula,
rachitis, &c., patience and persistent care are a *sine quâ non*,
it is doubtful if anyone would be bold enough, from the
comparatively limited number of observations at our disposal,
to lay down a clear indication for patients who should go south,
and those who should mount the Alpine heights. At present

the same can be said of the mountains as of the South—a variety of cases have improved in a most remarkable manner. It is also undoubtedly true that in the high altitudes some rapidly advancing symptoms have been arrested when scarcely any hope of a return to health could be held out by physicians.

Patients with the following diseases should, however, refrain from seeking health at high elevations:—

1. Diseases of the brain, heart, or large vessels.
2. Tendency to articular rheumatism.
3. Kidney diseases (during winter).
4. Acute inflammations of throat or larynx.
5. Some diseases of bladder or prostate.
6. Persons somewhat advanced in years should not visit the mountains, unless the circulatory system is sound.

In every instance the body should be clothed in flannel, a thin, fine texture for summer wear. No great coats or heavy mantles will then be necessary, except for driving or sitting out. Even the danger in summer evenings from a fall in temperature, or from change of wind, is by no means serious, for the dry atmosphere does not carry with it the chilliness and cold which is felt in climates where the absolute humidity is greater. Moreover, the concert room, salons, corridors, &c., within the Maloja hotel permit of in-door recreation, with ample breathing space, whilst in the *parc* and gardens, numerous *pavillons* afford shelter externally, the mind being enlivened by variety in amusements and magnificent scenery. There is no lack of walks or drives either in St. Moritz direction—passing the villages of Sils, Silvaplana, and Campfer, with their superb lakes, or down by the steep incline of the Maloja Kulm into the beautiful Bergell Valley.

MALOJA.	WIESEN.
Position.—Situated at the S.W. end of the Upper Engadine. Receives more sun than any other Alpine Station. No morning nor evening mist. The Kursaal is placed on the western side of the plateau, and in this situation escapes most of the valley draught (thalwind). Extremely picturesque scenery at this part of the Engadine. Mountain screen, 3,000 to 6,000 feet.	Wiesen is located on the hillside, the Landwasser being about 1,000 feet below the houses. The mountain screen ranges from 3,000 to 5,000 feet above. There is in fine weather no morning nor evening mist; a constant but imperceptible current of cold air travels down the declivities. Notwithstanding that this motion of the atmosphere is unfelt, it is sufficient to obviate any tendency to stagnation.
Proximity to Glaciers.—Partially surrounded by glaciers.* Bernina glaciers, W.; Murtel, 10 kilometres; Fedoz, Forno, and Albigna, 7 to 10 kilometres distant, on the S.W. and S. * The effects of glacial air on the respiration has been noted by Dr. Burney Yeo, who considers that its condensed state gives a sensation of freedom in breathing.—" Health Resorts and their Uses."	Scaletta, 13 miles to the E. (Small glacier.) Silvretta Glacier, 20 miles to N.E.
Pernicious Winds. — South-west wind. Fairly well sheltered from South wind. The sultry characters of the föhn appear to be extremely rare, probably from the influence of the surrounding glaciers.	South and south-west currents, know locally by the name of " föhn.'
Thalwind (valley wind).—Blows from the N.E. principally on the eastern side of the plateau, in a line with the Bergell valley, and is mostly noticed on the Kulm, about one mile distant from the hotel.	This wind, which blows in every Swiss valley, is infrequent, as the village is situated far above the bed of the gorge, and consequently out of the zone of commotion of air, caused by the descending cold currents which converge and flow down the gorges and ravines.

HEALTH RESORTS OF THE GRISONS.

Davos.	St. Moritz.
Situated on rising ground in the valley itself. The mountain screen ranges from 3,000 feet to 5,000 feet. The mist which sometimes covers the bed of the valley in the early morning, is soon dissipated by the sun, but the usual haze seen over villages and small towns is visible unless moved by wind.	The Kulm Hotel is about 300 feet above the lake. A thin mist hangs over the lake in the morning, but below the level of the dwellings. The aspect is more open than Davos, and there is more wind.
Scaletta, 8 miles to S.E. Silvretta, 12 miles N.E. by E..	Extensive Bernina glaciers to S. and S.W. Piz Bernina is 15 kilometres distant.
South and south-west winds, as at Wiesen.	South and south-west wind.
Thalwind is often felt between 2 and 3 p.m. from the N.E.	No regular valley wind, blowing from a definite direction, independently of the upper current. Nevertheless, the wind rises regularly in the course of the day, and is unpleasant from either the north or south (Mr. Waters' observations). Thalwind felt on the St. Moritz Kulm.

NUMBER OF HOURS OF POSSIBLE SUNSHINE DURING WINTER.

	Maloja.†	Wiesen.	Davos.	St. Moritz.*
1 Nov.	... $7\frac{1}{2}$ hours	$7\frac{1}{3}$ hours	... $7\frac{1}{3}$ hours	... — hours
15 „	... $6\frac{1}{4}$ „	— „	... — „	... 6 „
1 Dec.	... $6\frac{1}{2}$ „	... $5\frac{1}{4}$ „	.. $5\frac{1}{4}$ „	... $5\frac{1}{4}$ „
15 „	... $6\frac{1}{4}$ „	... $5\frac{1}{12}$ „	... $5\frac{1}{12}$ „	... $5\frac{1}{12}$ „
1 Jan.	... $6\frac{1}{10}$ „	... $5\frac{1}{6}$ „	... 5 „	... $5\frac{1}{12}$ „
15 „	... $6\frac{1}{3}$ „	... $5\frac{5}{6}$ „	... $5\frac{1}{2}$ „	... $5\frac{1}{3}$ „
1 Feb.	... $6\frac{5}{6}$ „	... $7\frac{1}{4}$ „	... $6\frac{1}{3}$ „	... $7\frac{1}{12}$ „
15 „	... $7\frac{1}{8}$ „	... $7\frac{2}{3}$ „	... $7\frac{3}{4}$ „	... $8\frac{1}{12}$ „

* Das Oberengadin (Dr. J. M. Ludwig).

† These observations were taken from one spot on the Maloja (The Kursaal); if the chalets or grounds of the hotel had been included, a very much larger duration of sunshine would be recorded.

MEAN DAILY TEMPERATURE AT 7 A.M., GIVEN IN DEGREES CENTIGRADE.

		Nov.	Dec.	Jan.	Feb.	Mean for the whole winter '83-84.
*Maloja	(6,000 ft.)	—3·2	—6·3	—6·5	—7.9	—5·9
†Wiesen	(4,771 ft.)	—1·5	—5·3	—3·3	—3·1	—3·3
†Davos	(5,105 ft.)	—3·7	—7·1	—5·9	—5·5	—5·5
†Andermatt	(4,738 ft.)	—3·4	—8·1	—5·5	—5·0	—5·5

* Calculated from the observations of M. Kuoni.

† Furnished to the author by Professor Billwiller, Director of the Meteorological Stations.

THE JOURNEY FROM ENGLAND.

The quickest route from London to the Maloja during winter is by Dover, Calais, Boulogne, Amiens, Tergnier, Laon, Rheims, Belfort, Bâle, and Coire.

The tidal boats from Folkestone to Boulogne are more agreeable to travel by, and the luggage by this route is taken care of, and not so roughly handled as between Dover and Calais. Inquiries must be made of the South-Eastern Railway Company for the hours of departure, as these boats depend on the tide.

Viâ Dover and Calais, a start is made at 10 a.m. or 8 p.m. from London. In the former case lunch can be obtained at Calais at 2 p.m., dinner at Tergnier at 6 p.m., and Bâle reached at 6 a.m., where breakfast is taken at the railway station. From Bâle the journey is continued, after breakfast, either to Como by the St. Gothard line, and from thence to Colico by steamer, then by diligence to Chiavenna and Maloja; or leaving Bâle at 7 a.m. Coire is reached at noon. (A stay of two hours can be made at Zürich, if desired, and Coire reached later.)

From Coire the diligence leaves in the early morning for Maloja, *viâ* the Julier Pass and Silvaplana.

It is advisable for delicate persons to break the journey either at Bâle or Coire. Those who are unable to obtain any sleep in a train would do well to alight at Bâle and go to bed; otherwise a break at Zürich for two hours, partaking of a dinner at one of the numerous hotels in that interesting town, will be sufficiently refreshing to allow of a continuation of the journey without fatigue. A telegram might be sent to Hôtel Steinbock, requesting a room to be warmed, as the air at Chûr will feel chilly in autumn after sitting still in the train. Should the weather be fine, a few days' stay can be made with benefit, previous to mounting. A private conveyance should then be taken for a short journey to Mühlen, spending the night there. From Mühlen the diligence leaves at 2 p.m. for Silvaplana, and Maloja is reached at 6 p.m.

Should the route by the St. Gothard railway be chosen (*viâ* Como, Colico, Chiavenna, Promontogno) the train leaves Bâle at 7.30 a.m. for Como, where the night is spent, after which the boat is taken to Colico, and diligence to Chiavenna, where another rest is made ; or an agreeable stay can be made at Promontogno, situated in a picturesque part of Val Bregaglia, and only four hours from Maloja (ascent).

METEOROLOGICAL OBSERVATIONS

TAKEN IN THE MALOJA.

BY

A. TUCKER WISE, M.D.

SUMMARY OF OBSERVATIONS

(Published in detail

	AT 9 A.M.						AT NOON.					
	Air Temperature.		Maximum.		Minimum.		Amount of Cloud.	Air Temperature.		Maximum.		Minimum.		Amount of Cloud.
	Fahr.	Centigrade.	Fahr.	Centigrade	Fahr.	Centigrade.	1 to 10.	Fahr.	Centigrade.	Fahr.	Centigrade.	Fahr	Centigrade.	1 to 10.
Nov. 1883	26.4	—3.1	44	6.7	11	—11.7	4	30.5	—0.8	43	6.1	15	—9.4	4
Dec. ,,	19.3	—7	45	7.2	—2	—18.3	4.1	25	—3.9	43	6.1	0	—17.8	4.2
Jan. 1884	19.3	—7	40	4.4	—4	—20	4	25.7	—3.5	39	3.9	0	—17.8	3.3
Feb. ,,	17.3	—8.1	37	2.8	—7.5	—22	4	26.5	—3	38	3.4	—2	—18.9	4.3
	20.6	—6.3	45	7.2	—7.5	—22	4	26.9	—2.8	43	6.1	—2	—18.9	4

Mean Temperature for the Winter = 25° Fahr. (— 3°.9 Centigrade).

Average weight of Moisture = 12 grains per 10 cubic feet of Air.

Average drying Power of Air = 5.4 grains per 10 cubic feet of Air.

Average daily quantity of Ozone, with 6 hours exposure (scale 0° to 20°) 7°.4.

Highest Maximum Thermometer = 45° Fahr. (7°.2 Cent.), 26th December.

Lowest Minimum Thermometer = — 7°.5 Fahr. (— 22° Cent.), 19th February.

Highest Solar Radiation = 143° Fahr. (61°.6 Cent.), 13th February.

FOR THE WINTER OF 1883-4

in the last Edition).

Weight of moisture in 10 cub. ft. of air.	Drying power of air per 10 cubic feet.	AT 3 P.M.						Amount of Cloud.	Force of wind.	Mean Solar Radiation.		Rain Gauge.	Snow.	Ozone,6hours exposure.
		Air Temperature		Maximum.		Minimum.								
		Fahr.	Centigrade.	Fahr.	Centigrade.	Fahr.	Centigrade.	1 to 10.	1 to 12.	Fahr.	Centigrade.	mm.	Centimetres.	1 to 10.
Grains.	Grains.													
14	6	30.5	−0.8	42	5.6	19.5	− 7	4	0.7	113	45	53.2	56	7
11	5.4	24.8	−4	43.5	6.4	7	−13.9	4.8	1	89	31.7	26.2	29.5	7
11	5.4	27.3	−2.4	41	5	13.5	−10.2	2.8	1.3	105	40.6	13.3	26.2	6.6
12.2	4.7	27.5	−2.5	38	3.3	15	− 9.4	4.3	0.7	108	42.2	21.4	34	9
12	5.4	27.5	−2.4	43.5	6.4	7	−13.9	4	0.9	104	40	114.1	145.7	7.4

The Maximum and Minimum Thermometers were noted three times a day, for the purpose of determining the variation of temperature during forenoon and afternoon.

The Dew-point and Weight of Vapour in the atmosphere were calculated from Glaisher's tables, in conjunction with Apjohn's formula:—

$$F = f \tfrac{d}{63} \times \tfrac{h}{30}$$

when the temperature of the wet bulb was above $32°$;

and $F = f \tfrac{d}{56} \times \tfrac{h}{30}$ when below $32°$ Fahr.

and the force of the wind noted according to the Beaufort scale, judged from the readings in miles, of an anemometer placed on high ground in an exposed part of the plateau, 14 feet above snow.

The "Drying Power of the Air," noted in the tables, is the weight of vapour which ten cubic feet of air were still capable of absorbing at the time of observation.

METEOROLOGICAL NOTES.

The winter of 1884-5, in the Upper Engadine, resembled the previous winter as regards the limited snow-fall for the months of November and December. Such a thin coat of snow had not been known for nearly forty years, and as the qualities of Alpine Winter Climate depend greatly on the depth of the early snow-covering, *typical* Alpine Winter did not make its appearance until about the middle of January. Sleighs could scarcely run, and although much fine weather was experienced, the snow was so light and powdery that it could be easily removed with the foot, and dust kicked up along with it from off the ground beneath. Owing to this condition many slopes and rocks were left bare, as in the preceding winter, favouring absorption of solar heat by the earth, to be again radiated off into space during the night, and in this way causing local movements of air.

The temperature in November closely followed the average of the year previous, viz. 29°·5; for November, 1884, 29°·1, for November, 1883, the highest maximum was 53°·8 Fahr.; against 41° Fahr., November, 1884. The lowest "minimum" 8° Fahr. and 11° for November, 1883. The months of January and February were on the whole colder than the last year. No rain fell during the whole winter. Fog was noted on four days in November, one for December, one for January, one for February, and five in March. The wet and dry bulbs indicated saturation on eleven days only. Hygrometric observations, although the most important in the study of climate, cannot, without the aid of the chemical hygrometer, be taken with precision at the lower temperatures. It is therefore doubtful if the calculations of "Weight of moisture," and "Drying power of air," are absolutely exact, but they approach as near correctness as possible with the means at our present command. I am in accord with my friend, Mr. A. W. Waters, who has had long experience of Alpine climate, that there is a point where August's Psychrometer fails to indicate accurately the humidity of the air.

It may be noticed that the "minimum" temperatures (which as a rule occur about 7 or 8 a.m.) are often considerably below the "Dew Point" of 9 a.m. on the same day and 3 p.m. of the day previous, without any fall of moisture occurring. As a partial explanation for this it may be inferred that in clear weather the upper strata of the atmosphere contain but an infinitesimal amount of watery vapour, the air having passed over extensive areas of land, and its moisture having been condensed by the frozen peaks which impede the course of aërial currents towards this part of Switzerland, in which case evaporation from the snow-covering of the country slowly supplies the lower stratum of air with moisture, evaporation from the snow increasing with rise of temperature and diminishing with the fall; and although the "Dew Point" throughout the day and in the evening is generally much higher than the "minimum" of the night no deposit of moisture takes place when the temperature falls, as the invisible vapour is dissipated into space, diffusion ensuing speedily with the lessened barometric pressure at these heights. That these climates contain an extremely small quantity of watery vapour in the air is a well-established fact, but the precise measurement presents a little difficulty. To illustrate the excessive dryness in the depth of winter the mean weight of moisture at noon in 10 cubic feet of air was but 9·1 grains for January; even this is probably too high a calculation, as the result was arrived at by the formula shown at page 93, which is not quite suitable for low temperatures. At Kew during the same month the mean, as given to me by G. M. Whipple, Esq., Superintendent of the Observatory, was 25 grains.

To the absence of moisture suspended in the air may be ascribed the capability of wild animals to support the cold in these high regions, and human beings the changes in temperature. It is by no means rare for individuals to quit a room and proceed out of doors with a difference of 50°, and occasionally 60° Fahr., without feeling any pressing need of gloves or extra clothing. On the bright days of mid-winter, surrounded by snow and ice, the new visitor marvels that the low temperature is unperceived, and that the sun's rays carry with them the heat of summer. Combined with dryness the cold restrains the life and development of micro-organisms in the external air; ordinary catarrh is almost unknown, except in badly ventilated houses, where a "cold in the head," or a "sore throat" seems liable to be communicated to others. During the whole winter at the Maloja no person suffered from the former complaint; and but two cases of sore throat occurred brought on through indiscreet exposure, although the daily average of persons inhabiting the Kursaal was between 60 and 70. It can be demonstrated that a drier layer of air surrounds animals and is inhaled by them in these climates, than in Egypt (which has generally been considered the driest air for consumptive patients). By respiration a rise in the temperature of the air takes place, and whatever the temperature inhaled may be, the exhaled air approaches that of the blood. On the other hand the atmosphere in immediate contact with the skin and between garments becomes warmed, consequently what would be expressed by a "relative" humidity of 90 per cent. at 26° Fahr. (the mean temperature for the winters 1884-5) becomes 8 per cent. near the temperature of the lungs, and 13 per cent. in contact with the body, if we calculate the air underneath the clothing at 80° Fahr.

In Egypt the "relative" humidity for the month of June, 1884, was 73, February 70, this has a drying power at the temperature of the body (say 98·6 Fahr.) of 160 and 156 grs. per 10 cubic feet, which is seen to be actually a less dry air when taken into the lungs than that of an Alpine height. Although I have mentioned the "*relative*" humidity for contrast, this observation in the comparison of cold climates with other places, requires a further calculation to afford a definite idea of the hygrometric state of the atmosphere, for with variation in the temperature the standard varies, and what may be a damp climate at 90 per cent. in one locality, is a dry climate in another with regard to animals, for at Cairo 90 per cent. relative humidity represents in January, 1884, 37 grains of vapour in 10 cubic feet, whereas at Maloja for the same month but 14 grains are suspended in the air at 90 per cent. Therefore, in a medical aspect there can be no hesitation in saying that the "*absolute*" humidity should on no account be neglected, the drying power of the air being given in grains of vapour, then some approximate estimate of evaporation from the lungs and skin might perhaps be made.

METEOROLOGICAL OBSERVATIONS

1884 Nov.	AT 9 A.M.				AT NOON.				Elastic Force of Vapour in In. of Mercury	Weight of Moisture in 10 cub. ft. of air	Dew Point.	Drying power of air per 10 cub. ft.
	Dry Bulb.	Wet Bulb.	Cloud.		Dry Bulb.	Wet Bulb.	Cloud.					
			Form.	Amount 0 to 10.			Form.	Amount 0 to 10.				
	Fahr.	Fahr.			Fahr.	Fahr.				Grains	Fahr.	Grains
1	35	31	blue	0	41.5	38.5	blue	0	.205	24	35.2	6
2	32.5	30	over	10	32	31	fog	10	.165	19	29.7	2
3	28.8	27	blue	0	37.3	33.5	blue	0	.157	18	28.6	7
4	31	27	cir	1	39.5	32	blue	0	.118	14	22	14
5	33.5	30	blue	0	43	35	blue	0	.131	15	24.4	17
6	31.8	27.4	blue	0	45	35	blue	0	.113	13	21	21
7	31	27.5	blue	0	46.6	36	blue	0	.115	14	21.4	22
8	36.6	31.2	blue	0	50	40.5	blue	0	.165	19	29.7	22
9	34.5	31.5	blue	0	47.2	40	blue	0	.181	21	32	16
10	37.2	32	cir	1	50	40	c.c.	5	.156	18	28.5	23
11	36.5	32.5	blue	0	45.8	37.5	blue	0	.149	17	27.3	18
12	34	31	blue	0	46	36	cir	1	.131	15	24.4	20
13	26	24	blue	0	25	25	fog	10	.135	16	25	0
14	22	20	blue	0	30	24.2	blue	0	.081	10	13.8	9
15	24	22	blue	0	35	26.5	blue	0	.066	8	9.5	16
16	21.8	19.6	blue	0	27.8	23	blue	0	.083	10	14.4	8
17	23.2	21.4	blue	0	26.5	24.5	blue	0	.115	14	21.5	3
18	23.8	21.2	c.c.	8	27.5	21.2	cum	8	.061	7	7.8	11
19	23	21.5	c.n.	8	25	21	cum	2	.079	10	13.4	6
20	14.6	12.6	c.c.	1	21	17.8	blue	0	.070	9	10.9	4
21	15.5	15	c.c.	5	22	18	c n.	6	.064	8	8.8	6
22	15.4	14.2	c.c.	2	19	18	blue	0	.089	11	15.8	1
23	17.8	16.2	c.c.	3	21	20	c.c.	4	.099	12	18.3	1
24	13.2	12	c.c.	2	16	13	blue	0	.053	6	4.5	5
25	17	15.5	c.c.	4	23.8	18.8	blue	0	.060	7	7.2	8
26	13.5	12	blue	0	23	19	blue	0	.069	8	10.5	6
27	21	20	blue	0	28	23	blue	0	.081	10	13.9	8
28	15.2	14	blue	0	29.6	23.8	blue	0	.079	10	13.4	9
29	22	21.8	sn.	10	22.8	22.2	sn.	10	.114	14	21.3	½
30	17	15	sn.	10	23	19.5	over	10	.075	9	12.3	5
	24.9			2.2	32.3			2.2		16.2		9.8

OF THE MALOJA. 101

AT 3 P.M.

Dry Bath.	Wet Bath.	Maximum.	Minimum.	Cloud.		Wind.			Solar Radiation.	Rain Gauge.	Snow.	Barometer. Corrected for Temperature.
				Form.	Amount 0 to 10.	Upper Current.	Lower Current.	Force 0 to 12.				
Fahr.	Fahr.	Fahr.	Fahr.						Fahr.		ctm.	m.m.
40.2	35	45	29.5	blue	0	NE	SW	1	109			
32	31	34	29.5	cum	9	SW	SW	0.5	80			
34.8	31	39.2	25.5	blue	0	NE	S	0.5	111			
38.7	32	41.8	24	blue	0	NE	SW	1	114			
46.1	41	47	23.5	blue	0	NE	NE	2	114			
44	39	46	25.5	blue	0	SW	SW	1	113			
45.6	36	48	25.5	blue	0	SW	W	0.5	114			
51	42	53.8	30	blue	0	NE	NE	1	114			623.3
51	42	53.5	30.5	blue	0	NE	NE	0	97			625.2
51.8	42	53	34	c.c.	2	N	SW	1	102			624.4
41	35.5	46.5	33	c.c. nim	9	SSW	SSW	0	65			623
45.3	36.3	47	30	blue	0	E	SW	0.5	115			620
24.5	24.5	26	21.5	fog	10	SW	SW	2	81			616.8
22	22	30.5	18	fog	10	NE	SW	1	92			617
34	25.5	36.5	17	blue	0	NE	W	1	102			617.5
27	24	28	15.5	blue	0	NE	NE	1	90			614.4
22	21.8	29	16	fog	10	SW	SW	1	90			613.7
24.8	21	27	14.5	c.n.	8	NW	SW	0.5	70			611.4
22.8	20.1	27.1	19.5	c.c.	2	W	W	2	98			612.7
22.2	19.2	24.2	12.5	c.c.	1	W	W	1	92			611.8
20	19.5	24	8	sn.	10	SW	SW	0.5	80		0.5	606.9
19	18	22.5	8	over	10	SW	SW	0.5	50		0.5	606.4
20.2	18	21	13.5	over	10	NE	SW	3	84			606.9
17.5	15	18.5	10.5	c.n.	8	W	W	1	85		0.5	611.8
23	20	25	10	c.n.	4	W	SW	0	70			613
24.8	20.5	26.5	10	blue	0	NE	NE	1	95			614.5
28	24	28.5	14	c.c.	4	NE	W	1	90			616
26.5	23	30	9	cir	2	NE	NE	1	91			613
22	22	23	20	sn.	10	SW	SW	1	51		1	607
22	19.5	26	8	sn.	10	SW	SW	0	50		4	605.3
31.4		53.8	8		4.3			0.9	90		6.5	

	AT 9 A.M.		Cloud.		AT NOON		Cloud.		Elastic force of Vapour in inch of Mercury	Weight of Moisture in 10 cub. ft. of Air	Dew Point.	Drying Pow. of Air per br. cub. ft.
	Dry Bulb.	Wet Bulb.	Form.	Amount 0 to 10	Dry Bulb.	Wet Bulb.	Form.	Amount 0 to 10				
	Fahr.	Fahr.			Fahr.	Fahr.				Grains.	Fahr.	Grains
1	7.5	7	c.	1	18.5	14.6	blue	0	.051	6	3.5	6
2	17.9	16.8	c.n.	7	20	18	blue	0	.081	10	13.5	3
3	18.5	17	c.	3	28.8	23.8	blue	0	.086	10	13	8
4	27	24	c.n.	3	28.2	23.6	blue	0	.086	10	13	8
5	23	21.5	over	10	25.5	22	blue	0	.088	11	13.5	5
6	28.8	27.5	over	10	33.5	30	blue	0	.137	16	23.5	6
7	30	29	st.	1	37.8	32	blue	0	.132	15	24.5	10
8	27.1	24	blue	0	31.8	29.8	blue	0	.140	17	27.4	3
9	29	28.8	over	10	28	28	fog	10	.153	18	28	0
10	24.2	21.5	blue	0	27.5	22	blue	0	.072	9	11.5	8
11	20.8	19	over	10	29.8	25	st.	1	.095	11	17.5	8
12	28.1	27.1	c.c.	4	35	30	c.c.	8	.125	15	23.4	9
13	28.8	23.5	cum	4	35	29	blue	0	.110	13	20.4	10
14	27.5	24.5	cum	1	36.5	32	c.	1	.143	17	26.3	7
15	27.5	25	c.c.	6	35	31	blue	0	.140	17	25.9	6
16	30	28	c.	6	33	30	c.c.	4	.142	17	26.2	5
17	27	26.8	sn.	10	27.2	27	sn.	10	.145	17	26.6	0
18	19.5	18	sn.	10	18.5	15	cum	3	.056	7	5.7	5
19	14	13	c.	1	27	21	c.	1	.063	8	8.5	9
20	22.5	22	sn.	10	21.2	20.5	sn.	10	.104	12	19.2	1
21	21.8	20	sn.	10	22.8	19.8	sn.	10	.082	10	14.2	4
22	20	19	cum	4	21.8	19	sn.	10	.079	9	13.3	4
23	20	19	over	10	25	22.8	sn.	10	.103	12	19.0	4
24	24.6	23	over	10	26.8	24.5	over	10	.112	13	20.8	4
25	12	11	c.n.	1	16	14	blue	0	.065	8	9.0	2
26	18	17	over	10	25	22.8	sn.	10	.103	12	19	4
27	14.8	14.4	blue	0	25	22	blue	0	.093	11	16.7	5
28	22.5	21.5	c.n.	5	26.5	25.5	sn.	10	.129	15	24	2
29	26.8	26.5	sn.	10	27	26.5	over	10	.139	16	25.6	1
7	12.2	12	c.	4	24	21	cum	6	.088	10	15.5	5
31	20.5	19.5	c.n.	4	22	20.4	blue	0	.096	11	17.5	3
	22.3			5.6	27			4		12.3		5

OF THE MALOJA. 103

				AT 3 P.M.			Cloud.		Wind.					
Dry Bulb.	Wet Bulb.	Maximum.	Minimum.	Form.	Amount 0 to 10.	Upper Current.	Lower Current.	Force 0 to 12.	Solar Radiation.	Rain Gauge.	Snow.	Barometer Corrected for Temperature.
Fahr.	Fahr.	Fahr.	Fahr.						Fahr.	Ctm.		m.m.
17	13.5	20	5	blue	0	NE	NE	1	90			608.8
23	20	23	−0.5	cum	3	W	W	0	81			611.4
28.2	24	29	8.5	c.n.	8	SW	SW	0.5	85			613.5
27.6	25	29	22	over	10	SW	SW	2	50			615
27.8	23.6	28	20	c.c.	2	W	W	0.5	65		4	614.2
35	31.8	37	18	blue	0	NE	SW	0.5	90		5	617.5
41	37	42	19	blue	0	NE	NE	0	96			620.8
29.8	28.8	36	20	blue	0	NE	NE	1	98			622.1
28	28	30	25.5	fog	10	SW	SW	2	50			620.3
27	22.5	29	22.5	c.n.	2	NE	NE	2	100	1		618.4
27.2	24	30.5	11.5	c.n.	4	SW	SW	2	97			616.7
33	29	36	17.5	c.n.	5	W	W	1	72		5	612.3
37	30	39.5	21	blue	0	NW	NW	1	85			622
36.8	32	40	24	c.	1	N	N	0	100			622.7
28.8	26	37	22.5	c.	2	NE	NE	1	85			618.3
32.2	29	35	23.5	c.n.	4	SW	SW	0.5	60			614.5
27	26.8	27	20.5	sn.	10	SW	SW	2	55			612
18.8	15	21	16.5	cum	1	W	W	2	60		10	613
27.3	23	29	10	n.	4	SW	SW	1	91			611.6
21.5	21	26	13	sn.	10	W	W	2	50		5	601
22	20	23	19.5	sn.	10	NW	NW	1	52		2	593
21	19	22	18	c.n.	4	E.	W	2	70			601.6
25.2	23.2	27	16.5	over	10	NE	SW	0	49			605
24.5	23	28	12	over	10	NE	W	0	40			606
18.5	16	20	9.5	over	10	NE	NE	1	45			605.3
22	21.8	27	11.5	sn.	10	SE	S	0	40			609.5
24.2	22	27	12.8	blue	0	NE	NE	0	80		5	615
26.8	26	29	8	sn.	10	S	S	0.5	62			615
26	25.8	27	24	cum	7	NE	NE	1	50		5	609.9
26.5	24.5	27	2	over	10	NE	NE	0	51			610.5
24.2	22	26	17	blue	0	NE	NE	0	85		3	615
27		42	−0.5		5			0.9	70		45	

METEOROLOGICAL OBSERVATIONS

1885 Jan.	AT 9 A.M.				AT NOON.						
	Dry Bulb.	Wet Bulb.	Cloud. Form.	Amount 0 to 10.	Dry Bulb.	Wet Bulb.	Cloud. Form.	Amount 0 to 10.	Elastic Force of Vapour in In. of Mercury	Weight, Moisture in 10 cub. ft. of Air.	Dew Point.	Drying Power of Air per 10 cubic feet
	Fahr.	Fahr.			Fahr.	Fahr.				Grains.	Fahr.	Grains.
1	14.5	13	blue	0	21	18	cir	2	.073	9	11.8	3
2	16.	15	fog	10	19	19	fog	10	.103	12	19	0
3	13.8	13.2	over	10	18.8	18.2	over	10	.094	11	17	1
4	10	9	blue	0	21.5	18	blue	0	.068	8	10	4
5	13.5	12	cir	3	19	17	blue	0	.077	9	12.8	2
6	6	5	blue	0	23	19	blue	0	.069	8	10.3	4
7	22	20	c.n.	8	23	20	cu	7	.083	10	14.3	3
8	4.5	3.8	blue	0	10	8.8	blue	0	.054	7	5	1
9	4	3	blue	0	15	12.2	blue	0	.051	6	3.5	3
10	8	7	blue	0	18	15	blue	0	.061	7	7.6	3
11	16.5	16	sn	10	18	18	sn	10	.098	12	18	0
12	4	3.5	blue	0	14	12	blue	0	.057	7	6	2
13	7	6	over	10	14.2	12	cum	8	.055	7	5.3	2
14	8.2	7.8	sn	10	10.8	9	over	10	.050	6	3	2
15	8.8	8	over	10	15	13.2	sn	10	.063	8	8.5	1
16	24.8	24.2	sn	10	26	24	sn	10	.112	13	20.9	2
17	19.8	18	over	10	26	24.2	over	10	.115	14	21.4	2
18	30	27.5	over	10	35	30.2	c.c.	6	.128	15	23.8	4
19	12	10.5	blue	0	22	19	blue	0	.078	9	13	3
20	8	7	blue	0	13	11.5	blue	0	.059	7	6.7	1
21	5	4	blue	0	17	13.5	cir	0	.050	6	3	3
22	4	3.5	blue	0	18.8	16	blue	1	.066	8	9.3	2
23	6.5	5.5	blue	0	18.5	16.3	blue	0	.072	9	11.4	2
24	−1	−1.5	blue	0	16.5	14	blue	0	.061	7	7.6	3
25	7	6	blue	0	18.8	15.2	blue	0	.056	7	5.7	3
26	3	2.5	blue	0	17.8	15	blue	0	.062	8	8	2
27	6	5	blue	0	18.5	15	blue	0	.056	7	5.7	3
28	14	12	blue	0	25.5	21	blue	0	.075	9	12.3	7
29	11.5	10.5	blue	0	25.8	22	blue	0	.086	10	15	6
30	6.7	6	blue	0	28.8	25	blue	0	.103	12	19	6
31	23	22.5	sn	10	27	26	sn	10	.132	16	24.5	1
	10·9			3.6	19.8			3.3		9.1		2.6

OF THE MALOJA.

AT 3 P.M.

Dry Bulb.	Wet Bulb.	Maximum.	Minimum.	Cloud. Form.	Cloud. Amount 0 to 10.	Wind Upper Current.	Wind Lower Current.	Force 0 to 12.	Solar Radiation.	Rain Gauge.	Snow	Barometer Corrected for Temperature.
Fahr.	Fahr.	Fahr.	Fahr.						Fahr.		ctm.	m.m.
20	17	24	9	blue	0	NE	NE	0	82			617.3
18.5	18.2	20	9.5	cum	8	s	s	0	45			616.2
22.8	21	24	9.5	over	10	NE	sW	0	35		½	615.4
21.5	17.8	23	4.5	blue	0	NE	NE	0.5	90			616.7
23	19	26	4.5	blue	0	NE	NE	0	88			615.6
20	17	24	0	blue	0	E	E	0.5	91			616.6
22	20	24	5.5	c.c.	9	s	NE	3	72			617
15	13	20	3	blue	0	NE	sW	0	85			615
20.2	16	23	−3	c.n.	4	NE	NE	0	88			611.4
20	17	24	4	blue	0	NE	NE	0	91			612
18.8	18	19	10	sn	10	sW	sW	2	50			605
15	12	19	2	blue	0	NE	NE	0.5	81		15	605
14.6	12.2	16	0	over	10	NE	W	1	40			599.4
12.2	10.3	12.5	6	over	10	W	W	1	45		2	598.3
16.2	15.5	16.5	−1	sn	10	NE	W	1	40			605.5
24.5	23.2	26.5	14.5	sn	10	sW	sW	0.5	50		5	606.3
31.5	28	32	11	over	10	W	E	1	60		30	611.4
33	29	36.5	17	cum	6	s	NE	0.5	85		2	612.7
20	17	25	8.5	blue	0	NE	NE	0	91			613
17.8	15	19	2	blue	0	NE	NE	0	86			612.6
21.6	13.5	24.5	−6.5	blue	0	NE	NE	0.5	87			610.4
21.5	15.5	24	1.5	blue	0	NE	NE	0	90			613.7
22	19	26	−1	blue	0	NE	NE	0	92			614.4
21	17	22.5	−5	blue	0	NE	NE	0	90			615.5
25	21	26	2.5	blue	0	NE	NE	0.5	90			614.3
21	18	25	−2	blue	0	E	NE	0	90			614
22	18	23	−1.5	blue	0	NE	NE	1	90			615.3
30.5	25.5	33	1.5	c.c.	4	NE	NE	0.5	92			618.3
28.5	25	31	3	blue	0	NE	NE	0	94			616.3
27.5	25	29.5	−4	cir	2	sW	sW	2	94			614.5
24.5	24	27.5	22	sn	10	sW	sW	1	54		5	611

METEOROLOGICAL OBSERVATIONS

1885 Feb.	AT 9 A.M.				At Noon							
	Dry Bulb.	Wet Bulb.	Cloud.		Dry Bulb.	Wet Bulb.	Cloud.		Elastic Force of Vapour in In. of Mercury	Weight of Moisture in 10 cub. ft. of Air.	Dew point.	Drying power of Air per 10 cubic feet.
			Form.	Amount 0 to 10.			Form.	Amount 0 to 10.				
	Fahr.	Fahr.			Fahr.	Fahr.				Grains.	Fahr.	Grains.
1	25.2	24.8	sn.	10	28.8	28	sn.	10	.146	17	26.9	1
2	17	16.8	fog	10	29.2	27.2	over	10	.131	15	24.4	4
3	29	28.8	sn.	10	33	33	sn.	10	.188	22	33	0
4	24.8	23.8	sn.	10	27	24.8	over	10	.115	14	21.5	3
5	7.5	7	c.c.	4	24.6	22	blue	0	.096	11	17.5	5
6	23.5	21.8	c.c.	4	30.5	26	blue	0	.103	12	19	7
7	6.5	5.5	blue	0	23.2	19.8	blue	0	.078	9	13	5
8	18	16.5	blue	0	29	24.5	cum	1	.094	11	17	7
9	9.5	9	over	10	25	22	over	10	.093	11	16.8	5
10	11.5	10	cum	1	23.5	19.5	cum	6	.071	8	11	7
11	11.8	10	blue	0	25	19.5	blue	0	.059	7	6.9	9
12	32	30	c.n.	7	35	31	sn.	10	.140	16	25.9	7
13	19	17	blue	0	27.8	23	blue	0	.083	10	14.4	8
14	4.5	3.2	blue	0	30.6	24.6	blue	0	.083	10	14.4	10
15	10	9	blue	0	30.3	25	blue	0	.090	10	16	9
16	26.5	23	over	10	31	29	over	10	.143	17	26.3	3
17	30	30	sn.	10	31	31	sn.	10	.174	20	31	0
18	29	28.5	sn.	10	32.2	31	sn.	10	.164	19	29.6	2
19	13	11.5	blue	0	34.5	27	blue	0	.084	10	14.5	13
20	28.5	28	sn.	10	30.5	29.5	sn.	10	.154	18	28.2	1
21	31	30	cum	6	42	38.5	cum	4	.201	23	34.7	7
22	24	23	blue	0	35.5	31.2	blue	0	.136	16	25.1	8
23	29.8	27	cum	5	33	30	cum	6	.142	17	26.2	5
24	21.8	20	blue	0	37.5	32	blue	0	.135	16	25.2	9
25	21.8	19.5	blue	0	37	31.8	blue	0	.135	16	25	9
26	28	25	blue	0	40	32	blue	0	.114	13	21.2	15
27	27	25.2	blue	0	41	32	blue	0	.106	12	19.6	17
28	24	22.5	cir	2	38	32	blue	0	.131	15	24.4	11
	20.8			4.2	31.6			4.1		14.1		6.6

OF THE MALOJA.

				Cloud.		Wind.					
Dry Bulb.	Wet Bulb.	Maximum.	Minimum.	Form.	Amount 0 to 10.	Upper Current	Lower Current.	Force 0 to 12.	Solar Radiation.	Rain Gauge.	Snow.	Barometer Corrected for Temperature.
Fahr.	Fahr.	Fahr.	Fahr.						Fahr.		Ctm.	m m.
27.2	27	29	19	sn.	10	SW	SW	1	57		8	615.5
30	29	32	15	fog	10	SW	NE	1	109		10	617
32	32	34.5	25	sn.	10	SW	SW	0	60		5	607.7
25	23	31	21	blue	0	SW	SW	1	107		40	606
27	24	32	—10	blue	0	SW	NE	0	120½			609.4
30	25.2	32	14	blue	0	N	NE	1	109			613.3
27	22	34.5	—4	blue	0	NE	NE	0	105			604.5
29.8	25	31.5	7	blue	0	N	NE	1	103			616.8
25	22	26	—8.5	sn.	10	SW	NE	1	69			610.5
23	19	26.5	8.5	over	10	N	NE	0.5	113		1	611.6
27.8	22.5	30	9	cum	4	N	N	0.5	115			615.5
32.8	28	37	19	cum	7	N	NNE	1	110		5	616.5
32.5	25	36	16.5	blue	0	N	SW	0.5	108			615.8
32	24.2	35.5	—5.5	cir	1	NE	SW	0	107			616
26.4	23	34	5.5	cum	6	NE	NE	0.5	100			615.6
32	30	33	7.5	cum	8	SW	SW	0.5	90			615
29	29	33	15	sn.	10	SW	SW	1	70		5	613.2
32.2	32	34	24	sn.	10	SW	SW	1	79		15	606.5
30.2	25.5	36.5	8	over	10	E	SW	1	127½		2	611.5
30	29	32	23	sn.	10	SW	SW	2	75		8	610.6
39	36.5	44	27	cum	1	W	SW	0	140		15	611.6
33	30.8	38	21	cum	1	N	NE	0.5	115			617.8
32	28	35	23	blue	0	N	NE	2	121			617.3
41	35.5	46	11	blue	0	NE	NE	0.5	118			621.5
42.8	33.8	47.5	12	blue	0	E	E	0	120			619.7
43	34.8	45	22	blue	0	E	E	0.5	115			621
45.5	38	46	18	blue	0	E	E	0.5	114			619.6
38.5	32.5	43	16	cir	2	S	NE	0.5	119			615.2
32		47.5	—10		4.3			0.7	103.4	114		

1885 Mar.	AT 9 A.M.				AT NOON			Elastic Force of Vapour in in. of Mercury	Weight of Moisture in 10 cub. ft. of air	Dew Point.	Drying power of air per 10 cub. ft.
	Dry Bulb.	Wet Bulb.	Cloud.		Dry Bulb.	Wet Bulb.	Cloud.				
			Form.	Amount 0 to 10.			Form.	Amount 0 to 10.				
	Fahr.	Fahr.			Fahr.	Fahr.			Grains.	Fahr.	Grains.
1	30	29	cum	5	32.5	29	cum	2	.130	15	24.2	6
2	25.8	24.5	cum	4	33	28	blue	0	.111	13	20.6	9
3	12	10	blue	0	29	25	cum	4	.101	12	18.6	7
4	25.5	25.5	sn.	10	27	26.5	sn.	10	.139	16	25.6	1
5	27.8	26	over	10	33	30.5	over	10	.149	17	27.4	5
6	33	32	sn.	10	32.5	32	sn.	10	.176	20	31.3	1
7	24.8	23	blue	0	39	32	blue	0	.122	14	22.8	13
8	20	19	cir	1	36	31	blue	0	.132	15	24.5	9
9	30.5	30.5	fog & sn.	10	31.5	31.5	fog & sn.	10	.177	20	31.5	0
10	30.2	29	cum	6	40	33	blue	0	.124	15	23.2	13
11	24	23	cum	4	34.5	31	cum	3	.144	17	26.5	6
12	28.2	26	cir	2	36.8	31	blue	0	.125	15	23.3	10
13	17.5	16	blue	0	30.1	25.9	blue	0	.105	12	19.5	7
14	26.5	25	blue	0	33	27	blue	0	.097	12	18	10
15	21	19	blue	0	31	27.3	blue	0	.118	14	22	6
16	21.5	18.8	blue	0	37.2	30	blue	0	.107	13	20	12
17	21.2	20	blue	0	38.5	30.5	blue	0	.104	12	19.2	14
18	25	24	fog	10	27	25.5	sn.	10	.138	15	23.5	2
19	29.8	28	sn.	10	36.2	33	sn.	10	.158	18	28.8	7
20	25.2	24	blue	0	39.8	34.8	blue	0	.156	18	28.5	10
21	34.5	31	c.c.	1	42.5	32	c.c.	4	.093	11	17	21
22	30.2	29	cum	5	35	30	cum	3	.125	15	23.3	8
23	30	29	sn.	10	33	31	sn.	10	.156	18	28.5	4
24	13.5	12	cum	4	14.5	12	cum	3	.054	6	5	4
25	11	10	over	10	18.8	16.8	cum	8	.076	9	12.5	3
26	25	23.5	cum	1								
	24.7			4.3	32.8			3.8		14.4		7.5

OF THE MALOJA.

AT 3 P M

Dry Bulb.	Wet Bulb.	Maximum.	Minimum.	Cloud.		Wind.			Solar Radiation	Rain Gauge.	Snow.	Barometer Corrected for Temperature.
				Form.	Amount.	Upper Current.	Lower Current.	Force 0 to 12.				
Fahr.	Fahr.	Fahr.	Fahr.						Fahr.		ctm.	m.m.
30	29	35	26.5	over	10	NNE	NNE	3	112			611.5
33	28	37	19	cum	1	NW	W	0.5	113			612
28.5	25	34	4	cum	5	SW	SW	2	110			611
29	27.8	32	7.5	over	10	SW	SW	1	77		1	611.7
32.2	31	34	3.5	over	10	W	SW	2	110		2	611
32	32	34	29	fog	10	W	W	1	60			603.6
40	33	44	21	c.n.	2	W	NE	0	143.5		9	611.5
34	31	38	11	c n.	2	SW	NE	1	123			616.4
31.8	31.8	33	29	fog & sn.	10	SW	SW	4	96		5	613.7
38.4	33	42.5	23.5	cum	1	SW	NE	4	132		5	612.5
32	30.5	42	20	sun-fog	10	W	NE	0.5	127			616
40.2	33	41.5	24	blue	0	NE	NE	0.5	122			615
39.5	32	40	13	blue	0	E	E	2	118.5			614.7
32.5	29	36	17	cir	2	N	NE	2	115			614
30.2	27.2	35	13	cum	3	SW	SW	0.5	113			617
41.5	32	42	10	blue	0	E	E	0	119			621.5
36.5	32	40	10	blue	0	NE	NE	0.5	115			618
29	26.5	29	8	sn.	10	SW	SW	2	122			613.5
30.8	30	39	23.5	over	10	SW	NE	1	140		10	609.2
40	33.4	43	17.5	blue	0	E	SW	0	127			610.2
45	33	48	18	cir	1	SW	N	0.5	128			610.2
35	31	38	21	c.n.	9	SW	SW	0.5	121.5			608.5
34	32.5	36	20	fog	10	SW	SW	2	130		12	607
14	12	33	11	cum	8	NW	NW	4	107			607
27	24	27.5	5	cum	8	E	NE	3	109		1	605.8
			15			E	E					610

| 33.4 | | 48 | 3.5 | | 5.2 | | | 1.5 | 115.6 | | 45 | |

HYGROMETRIC COMPARISON OF THE MALOJA WITH EGYPT.

	Mean Temperature.	Weight of Moisture in 10 cubic feet of Air.	Drying Power of Air at the Mean Temperature of the Atmosphere for 10 cubic feet.	Drying Power of Air at the Body Temperature, for 10 cubic feet.
	Fahr.	Grains.	Grains.	Grains.
*Egypt.—				
January, 1884	50.5	30	11	160
February, ,,	54.5	33.6	14.4	156.4
November, ,,	63.5	40.3	23.7	149.7
December, ,,	58	38.3	15.7	151.7
January, 1885	54.5	32.6	15.4	157.4
February, ,,	57	33.2	18.8	156.8
Means	56.3	34.6	16.5	155.3
† Maloja.—				
January, 1884	25.7	11	5.4	179
February, ,,	26.5	12.2	4.7	177.8
November, ,,	32.3	16.2	9.8	173.8
December, ,,	27	12.3	5	177.7
January, 1885	19.8	9.1	2.6	180.9
February, ,,	31.6	14.1	6.6	175.9
Means	27.1	12.5	5.6	177.5

* Calculated from eight observations during the twenty-four hours. (L'Observatoire Khédivial du Caire.)

† Calculated from the noon observations.

SUMMARY OF METEOROLOGICAL OBSERVATIONS TAKEN AT MALOJA DURING THE WINTER 1884-5.—By A. TUCKER WISE, M.D.

Month	9 A.M.		Noon.				3 P.M.				Force of Wind.	Solar Radiation.	Snow.
	Temperature.	Cloud.	Temperature.	Cloud.	Weight of Moisture in 10 cub. ft. of Air	Drying Power of Air in grs.	Temperature.	Maximum.	Minimum.	Cloud.			
	Fahr.		Fahr.				Fahr.	Fahr.	Fahr.			Fahr.	ctm.
November, 1884	24.9	2.2	32.3	2.2	16.2	9.8	31.4	53.8	8	4.3	0.9	90	6.5
December, ,,	22.3	5.6	27	4	12.3	5	27	42	−0.5	5	0.9	70	45
January, 1885	10.9	3.6	19.8	3.3	9.1	2.6	21.7	36.5	−6.5	3.6	0.6	76	59
February, ,,	20.8	4.2	31.6	4.1	14.1	6.6	32	47.5	−10	4.3	0.7	103.4	114
March, ,,	24.7	4.3	32.8	3.8	14.4	7.5	33.4	48	4	5.2	1.5	115.6	45
	20.7	4	28.7	3.5	13.2	6.3	29.1	53.8	−10	4.5	0.9	91	269.5

Mean Temperature for the Winter = 26° Fahr.
Average Weight of Moisture = 13.2 grains per 10 cub. ft. of Air.
Average Drying Power of Air = 6.3 ,, ,, ,,
Highest Maximum Thermometer = 53.8 Fahr. (8th November).
Lowest Minimum Thermometer = −10° Fahr. (5th February).
Highest Solar Radiation = 143°.5 Fahr. (7th March).

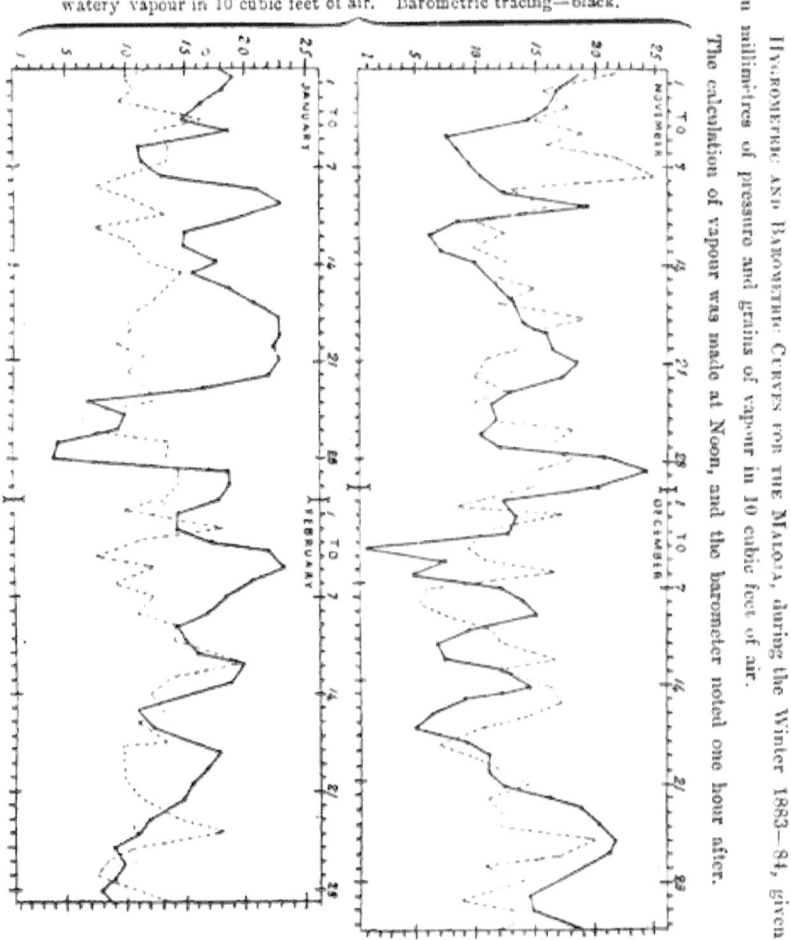

Millimètres for barometer. The same numbers indicate in grains the quantity of watery vapour in 10 cubic feet of air. Barometric tracing—black.

Hygrometric and Barometric Curves for the Maloja, during the Winter 1883–84, given in millimètres of pressure and grains of vapour in 10 cubic feet of air. The calculation of vapour was made at Noon, and the barometer noted one hour after.

ATTRACTIONS
IN THE
NEIGHBOURHOOD OF THE MALOJA.

ATTRACTIONS IN THE NEIGHBOURHOOD OF THE MALOJA.

No part of Switzerland offers a greater variety in attractions and easy excursions. The elevation of the Engadine permits the ascension of some of the highest peaks and glaciers in Switzerland without much difficulty.

The chief objects of interest which surround the valley are as follows:—

The Forno Glacier. A splendid glacier; 2 hours distant. Take the road westward of the Kursaal in the direction of the ornamental châlets, pass the Osteria Vecchia, keeping on the main road until the Maloja Kulm is reached. In front of Hôtel Kulm is a rock, with an iron railing on it, from whence a magnificent view may be obtained of the Bergell Valley. This point of view is only excelled by that seen from the Château Belvedere, on the hill to the right and hidden by the Mont des Chèvres, to be described further on. Following the main road again to its first turning, a bridle path is taken in the direction of Piz Rossi (the peak with a small glacier on the face of it beyond which, and to the right is seen a small snow-capped angle of the Cima di Rosso). Descend in a south-westerly direction, cross a small bridge over the river Ordlegna and follow the road to the left, after about 50 minutes the **Lac de Cavloccio**, is reached. This lake is remarkable for its placid waters and its curious green shade. A somewhat rugged path leads in the direction of Muretto when, on emerging from the gorge, the Forno Glacier is seen on the right hand, the best path to which, must not be taken too high on the mountain side.

Monte Sissone, from whence is a fine view of **Monte della Disgrazia** (12,000 feet).

Monte Rosso (9,800 feet).
Monte Forno (10,546 feet).
Monte Muretto (10,197 feet).
Monte della Disgrazia (12,057 feet).

All difficult, especially Disgrazia; but within ordinary reach of mountaineers.

Piz Margna (10,354 feet), with a steep glacier, 4 or 5 hours. A good view obtained of the snow-clad peaks of Monte del Forno, Rosatsch, Fex, Bernina, Morteratsch, &c.

Piz Corvatsch (11,345 feet), fronting Silvaplana, 9 or 10 hours. From the summit is seen an imposing view of the Bernina group, the valley of the Engadine, the Roseg Glacier, and nearly all the higher peaks of Switzerland.

Piz Surlej (10,456 feet), 7 or 8 hours.
Piz Julier (11,106 feet), 7 or 8 hours.

The Forno Pass. Over the Forno Glacier to St. Martino in the Val di Masino, 5 hours, difficult.

The Muretto Pass (8,389 feet). Approached by taking the route on the left bank of the river Ordlegna up to near the base of Monte Rossi which we leave on the right, 8 or 9 hours to Chiesa.

From Chiesa, (4,282 feet), to Sondrio, the capital of the Valtellina, and from thence to Colico, returning to Maloja by Chiavenna and the Bergell Valley. Poschiavo can also be reached by crossing the Canciano Pass from Chiesa, or Sils, by the Tremoggia Pass (9,900 feet) and the Fex Glacier, or Pontresina, over the Scerscen and Capütschin passes.

The Val Malenco is well worthy of a visit, and also the Valtellina, famous for its wine of which there is so large a consumption in Switzerland.

The Muretto Glacier. Near the summit of the Pass, 3 hours from Lac Cavloccio. Splendid view of Monte della Disgrazia, Forno, Sissone, Rosso, &c.

Monte Salicina, situated S.S.W. of Maloja, 4 or 5 hours distant. View obtained from the summit, of the Val Bregaglia and the mountains of Lombardy, &c.

Piz Lissone, a prominent peak to the W.S.W., 5 to 6 hours distant. The Piz Duan is seen to the right and behind this peak, the Gletscherhorn still further to the right.

The Septimer Pass (7,582 feet). One of the oldest historical routes traversed by the Romans. Descend from Maloja Kulm into the Bergell Valley and bear to the right behind Lunghino, crossing the Valle di Campo on its old paved military road.

Piz Longhinus (9,100 feet), W.S.W. of the Kursaal, where the Danube, the Po, and the Rhine take their sources. 3 hours from Maloja.

Fourcla da Lunghino. A pass leading into the Septimer and Forcellina to the Avers Valley.

Piz Gravasalvas (9,500 feet), 4 or 5 hours, difficult. To the N.W. of the Kursaal. Septimer Pass to the N.W., and N.

Motta Rotundo (8,100 feet), 3 hours. To the N. of the Kursaal.

Piz Materdell (9,700 feet), 4 or 5 hours distant. N.N.E. of the Kursaal.

Piz Lagrev (9,721 feet). The rugged pointed peak to the N.E., very difficult and dangerous to mountaineers unaccustomed to rock-work. 7 or 8 hours.

Piz Pulaschin (9,898 feet), N.E. of Lagrev, 5 or 6 hours. From many of the peaks can be seen a panorama of entire Switzerland—Mont Blanc, Tödi, Russein, Finsteraarhorn, Monte Rosa, Jungfrau, &c.

If desired, carriages conduct one near the paths of ascent, and, with the assistance of guides, the interesting points of view can be attained. For delicate persons or others who do not care to make ascents, more or less difficult, there are in the neighbourhood, several pleasant walks.

Casaccia. A small village at the junction of the Septimer and Forcellina Passes. Descend the zig-zag road after passing Maloja Kulm. The ruins of a church, St. Gaudenzio, said to have been constructed in the fourteenth century, are seen on the right, before entering the village. Time required from Maloja to Casaccia about 50 minutes.

The Cascade de l'Ordlegna, 25 minutes distant. When illuminated at night produces a startling effect. Situated half-way down the zig-zag road to Val Bregaglia, a directing post indicates the path to the Falls which are 5 minutes distant from the main road.

Belvédère. 15 minutes distant. Take the road to the N.W. of the Osteria Vecchia and follow its windings. From the rear of the Château is obtained one of the most magnificent views in the whole of Switzerland, far surpassing anything in the Engadine. On the left the Muretto Pass, leading to the Val Malenco (8 or 9 hours) and Valtellina. In front the picturesque Bergell Valley enclosed by high jagged mountains. To the right the Septimer Pass and Piz Lunghino; on the latter mountains are the sources of three great rivers, the Inn, the Maira, and Oberhalbstein Rhein, which take their rise here, and respectively flow into the Danube, the Po, and the Rhine.

Chemin des Artistes. This most charming of walks is on the western side of the Belvedere, winding between huge rocks and pines, away to the Val Pila (45 minutes). The most varying and romantic scene is passed, and many objects of interest present themselves, amongst which are the Gletschermühle, the track of the stone-avalanches from the Lunghino, the Falls of the Inn, the serrated peaks of Val Bregaglia, and the zig-zag road leading to Casaccia.

Colline du Chateau. This hill is approached by crossing the wooden bridge to the right of the Belvedere. On its summit a different view is obtained of all the points of interest mentioned in the last route, as well as a view of the Maloja Lake, stretching away to Sils Maria and shut in by the Bernina and Albula chains.

Lac de Cavloccio, 50 minutes, *ride* route to Forno Glacier.

Sils Baselgia, 50 minutes. A little village, situated in a wild and picturesque spot, at the N.E. end of the lake.

Sils Maria, 1 hour. At the entry of the valley of Fex, surrounded by hills covered with larches and red pines.

Crestalta, about 2 hours distant. Extensive view from the summit of a cone of the lakes of Sils and Silvaplana, with the Maloja plateau on one hand and St. Moritz on the other.

Chasté. In front of Maloja at the opposite end of the lake, on an islet where are found the ruins of an ancient castle.

Isola. A small hamlet seen on the S.E. side of the lake. The falls formed by the water from the Fedoz Glacier are 5 minutes from the village. A quaint old house with curious paintings on the walls, is open to strangers for view. Take the road S.E. of Kursaal, passing the group of châlets named Cresta. The walk, a very beautiful one, will occupy about an hour.

Crap da Chüern. An enormous perpendicular rock, crowned with forest, dominating the lake and forming a high precipice. It may be ascended from the road by passing to the left and behind. Time required, about 1¼ hours from hotel.

Platz de la Peninsule, 25 minutes distant. Situated at the base of the Crap da Chüern, covered with rocks and pines, Fedoz Glacier to the south. Following the main road the little valley of **Gravasalvas** opens out from the Lake of

Sils. The villages of Gravasalvas and Blaunca are situated here, and Lac Nair (8,000 feet) is gained from the valley.

Val Pila, 15 minutes. A hidden green valley at the base of Lunghino, the path to which is on the right hand side of the quarry. A return journey can be made by traversing the valley and mounting towards the Belvedere.

Lac Lunghino, 2 hours. Situated to the N.W. of the Hotel Kursaal, in the saddle formed by Piz Lunghino and Piz Gravalsalvas.

Lac Nair (8,000 feet). May be reached from the main road in the direction of the Crap da Chüern. A path will be discovered on the left about half a mile from the Hotel.

Fedoz Glacier. Between Piz Margna and Piz Güz (10,397 feet) is seen from near Isola and from the main road leading to Sils.

Fex Glacier. In continuation with the Val Fex at Sils Maria. A carriage takes one near the Glacier.

Ordeno, 30 minutes. A group of chalets situated on a grassy plateau overlooking the banks of the river Ordlegna. The continuation of the route on this side of the river leads to the Muretto Pass.

Albigna Water-fall. Seen from below Casaccia before entering Vicosoprano.

Gravasalvas, 1 hour. After passing Capolago, the village in front of the Kursaal, a road branches off at the first rivulet which leads to Gravasalvas. On the road are Spluga and Buera, hamlets secreted from the outer world, in the massive clefts of the Albula range. By branching off at Buera, the second village, and pursuing the track along the banks of the Ova del Mulin, Blaunca is reached. From this small cluster of habitations, there is also a mountain path to Gravasalvas and from thence to the main road, where the return to the Maloja, will occupy about three-quarters of an hour.

PROMONTOGNO.

A short promenade of 30 minutes can be made by taking the path on the S.E. of the Kursaal, passing through the hamlet of Cresta, and making for the church, after a few windings one emerges by the Osteria Vecchia. Longer walks in the direction of St. Moritz or down the Val Bregaglia towards Promontogno, are available, and in winter the descent on a toboggan to Vicosprano, and even Promontogno (12 miles) is easily made. The charms of these winter excursions in the glistening snow and brilliant sunshine, with deep blue sky, are unknown to summer visitors. In winter, also, good skating can be had, both on the Maloja Lake (3 miles long), and on the ice rink at the rear of the Hotel.

Distances.

Chiavenna to Samaden and Pontresina by the Val Bregaglia and Maloja Pass :—

	Miles.
Chiavenna	0
Castasegna	6
Promontogno	2
Stampa	2
Borgonouvo	1
Vicosoprano	2
Casaccia	$4\frac{1}{2}$
MALOJA (Kursaal)	4
Sils	$3\frac{1}{2}$
Silvaplana	3
Camfèr	$1\frac{1}{2}$
St. Moritz	3
Cresta	$0\frac{2}{3}$
Celerina	$0\frac{1}{4}$
Samaden	2
Pontresina	$3\frac{1}{2}$

www.ingramcontent.com/pod-product-compliance
Lightning Source LLC
Chambersburg PA
CBHW022130160426
43197CB00009B/1220